Third Edition June 1975
Second Edition March 1975
First Edition January 1975
Copyright © by *Petros Kogiones*
Printed in Greece by *Daskalakis Printing*

PETROS'
Famous Recipes

(An Adventure In Greek Cooking)

By PETROS KOGIONES

Cover and drawings by
Michael Nikolinakos

Published by *The Greek Press*
Chicago, Illinois

To Liz the beautiful lady with Love, Petros

DEDICATED

to the millions of wonderful Grecian housewives who relayed from mother to daughter the eternal tradition in Greek cookery and brought it to the excellence it stands today for the enjoyment of us all.

Cookery became an art, a noble science :
Cooks are gentlemen.

Robert Burton : Democritus to the Reader.

FOREWORD

When Petros asked us to write a foreword for his book on Greek cooking, our thoughts fled back twelve years to happier and simpler days, when for the first time we experienced both Greek food and Petros Kogeones. Dianna's was a few tables behind a grocery store on South Halsted Street in Chicago. Well-prepared orders of food came directly from the kitchen to the table, where already good Greek wine was filling one with the "Greek feeling." Then Petros as the best Ambassador of Greece to America, provided the final experience for his honored guests. A special occasion was remembered with song and wine; a spellbinding Greek dance punctuated with the crash of wine bottles transported one back to Greece itself; a simple glass of ouzo was offered as an expression of personal gratitude for YOUR being there. Dianna's has become for ourselves and for many a home away from home, a place of refreshment for both the human and spirit; God's gift to Chicago and the U.S.A.

We are overjoyed that Petros has decided to share all the benefits of his experience as providing the best Greek cooking for Chicago, if not for the Midwest and Nation. It has been our feeling for some time, as devotees of all things Greek, that a cookbook was needed containing dishes reflecting Greek cooking as prepared by Greeks, native to their homeland. But still recipes that any non-Greek cook can prepare easily to give friends a true Greek experience. We hope this cookbook will bring you a little of the excitement and discovery of Dianna's.

While the personal experience of Petros and his restaurant cannot be replaced for those of us who have become "Cousins" of the Kogeones family, this book will serve as a lasting remembrance and as a means for continuing what we have learned from the Kogeones about the glories of Greek cookery. For you, who have never experienced Petros and things Greek, the recipies will give the priviledged opportunity to experience at a distance what we in Chicago have come to honor and love. When you have created your masterpiece, the spirit of Petros will be there as you, your family, and your friends shout: OPAA in satisfaction over the Greek moment made possible by this book.

> The Professors:
> Dr. Rita C. Kucera
> Dr. Robert J. Kovarik

CHICAGO STATE UNIVERSITY
December 17, 1974

INTRODUCTION

There are many spirits of Greece, her art, her drama, her democracy, her philosophy. There is another: the spirit of her cooking. That, in its uniqueness and variety, I wish to honor by this book. Indeed, in speaking of the happy man, the great Aristotle says "Our bodies must be healthy and have food and other attention."

In the most difficult hours of their long and distinguished history, the Greeks never failed to understand that good food and Dionysian drink, the bonds of genuine friendship and the joyful pleasures of humble existence, are necessities of life. So in this tradition I bring to all of you who have been so lucky to discover my restaurant the very best of Greek cookery. This has become for me a labor of love.

In Dianna's Opaa I have taken the theme of the Greek goddess of the hunting, Diana. In the Greek myth, there was an enclosed valley filled with cypress and pines, containing a hidden cave with pure and sparkling waters. Although Diana loved to roam the mountains and the valleys of Arcadia tackling wild beasts or pursuing the light-footed roebuck, she would pause beside the clear waters of the fountain and bath with her companions until the waters refreshed her. The cave became the refuge from the world outside. My restaurant, Dianna's Opaa, like the valley with its cave, is a haven for those few who have a superior intelligence and a keen appreciation of the finer things of life. Even the rugged Diana, the sister of Apollo, permitted herself the gentler amusements like music and warm associations. I have followed her example in all I do.

Now in these pages I wish to share with you Greek cooking as prepared in my homeland and at my restaurant. My satisfaction has always come from seeing patrons leave my restaurant released from worldly cares and with a spirit of happiness. It is my ardent hope that the use of this book, with the secrets of Dianna's kitchen, will have the same result. As I have often said, "Welcome to my house and share my nectar and ambrosia." This you will now be able to say to your treasured friends!

Dianna's philosophy and that of this cookbook is a simple one, at the very core of the Grecian outlook. The Greeks possessed a firm belief in the worth of the individual man to be treated with honor and respect just because he is "he himself." In history the Greeks have displayed a sense of personal achievement, a man's obligation to make the most of his natural gifts: anything worth doing is worth doing well. As I have followed this in personally overseeing the results of my kitchen, so I have taken care to choose the very best of Greek dishes for your benefit.

In return for your patronage and support, I want to give you a lasting part of Dianna's restaurant: this collection of Greek recipes. By your preparation of these dishes, you enter into the company of the heroes of the Greek past, you become part of the Greek heritage and tradition which have for centuries so enchanted the imagination of men.

In your kitchen my spirit and that of Dianna's Opaa will surround you. Do not forget that I eagerly await word of your Greek experience when next you come as honored guest and true friend to dine with us. May that be soon!

                    With affection and best wishes,
                    Your Host,
                    Petros

PART I: *WELCOME*

"All creatures of the land,
The air and sea,
And every infant born
Or fruited tree,,
Earth Mother, is your child,
Your progeny!

Hesiod

DISCOVERING PETROS

Who is Petros?

No one can really tell you.

You have to discover him for yourself.

If you like the new and the exciting—and everyone alive does—you will start for *Petros' limeri* as soon as dusk comes to Chicago.

Petros' limeri or hideout is at *Dianna's Opaa* at 212 South Halsted Street, Chicago, Illinois, U.S.A.

Diana is the goddess of hunting, as you know from your mythology. Diana lived in the green mountains of Arcadia in Greece. Until she met *Petros*.

Petros comes from a nearby village, the Nestani, at the foothold of Artemision mountain where Diana was born.

When Diana met tall, slim and handsome *Petros,* she immediately fel in love with him. You see, *Petros* is a *leventis*, something like a demi-god.

Of course, for *Petros* too, Diana was love at first sight. They eloped and, pronto, came to Chicago.

In matters of love, heart is of necessity involved and *Petros* brought Diana to the heart of America that Chicago is. And he selected the heart of Chicago to establish his *limeri*.

At Dianna's Opaa you'll find *Petros*. You cannot miss him. His personality sparkles all over the place. He will greet you and give you the traditional *filoxenia* of the Greeks.

The dictionary says *filoxenia* means hospitality. To the Greeks and *Petros*, the word also means what it says: Love for the stranger, because the stranger is a friend.

After all, as one of the thousands upon thousands of enthusiasts wrote to *Petros*, Dianna's Opaa is God's gift to Chicago. If he means that at Dianna's Opaa you are wined and dined like a God, he is right. You get all that and much more at *Petros*'s headquarters.

For instance, if you are a pretty girl—and all girls are pretty—*Petros* will greet you with a kiss. Even if you are escorted.

Petros kiss is your appetizer. And, do not despair. You'll get another kiss from him for dessert.

Petros kisses an average of 1358 pretty girls a week. He is the world's champion kisser and no one can get close to him. Who else, really, is destined by Gods to kiss 1358 pretty girls a week?

No one. *Petros* was granted this privilege because *Petros* is one of a kind. He is unique. Like Dianna's Opaa is unique.

You have to come to Dianna's Opaa to find out who *Petros* is. We cannot tell you. Words cannot describe *Petros*. Because *Petros* means something different to every young man and every young girl. And we are all young at Dianna's Opaa. When you come you will experience it. An experience you never had before.

And then, you'll come back. For more . . .

A.

WHAT NICK MATSOUKAS SAYS ABOUT PETROS

"From The Streets Of Athens"

The "Windy City" was once justly called by Carl Sandburg, *"the hog butcher of the world."* It is the Second City, like Salonica is to Greece. I remember Chicago when Michigan Avenue was at the edge of the waterfront of Lake Michigan. It is grown. It build the world's largest building so that no longer will New York carry that dubious distinction as having the tallest skyscraper in the world. The skyscraper and its modern architecture features are Chicago made, and nobody can claim, otherwise. I have lived it. I have suffered it! I was happy! My years in Chicago were bitter-sweet. And because Chicago is more than a city to me, I have made my own population census of the *"hog butcher of the world."* You don't have to accept it but I stand by it with all my might.

Chicago is inhabited by people of all races and nationalities, all Americans. It is populated by Greeks and infested by Ahepans. The biggest number of the Greeks in Chicago must be Tripolitsotes. But Chicago also has *Petros*.

Now those outside of Chicago who don't know who *Petros* is, do me a favour and read the rest of this yarn and you might get an inkling of an idea who *Petros*, "the son of man" is.

Petros was born in Nestani, Tripolis in Arcadia. He is one of nine children, five boys and four girls. And he grew and grew. Now he is 6 feet two inches tall. *Petros* continued his school days career by attending the High School in Tripolis where the best "patsa" in the world is being served daily at the sub basement restaurant "O Yieros To Moria." After the High School years he got his diploma from the Pedagogical Academy of Tripolis. Then he went to the army and served as a lieutenant. And with the military past behind him he left for the land of opportunity where it "rains" dollars. And he too fell in line and opened up a restaurant Dianna's Restaurant "OPAA." With his brothers Ted, Peter, George and Demos they managed to make their "OPAA" Spa at 212 South Halsted Street one of the ten best eating establishments in the Windy City. That is the dictum of some experts who are supposed to know what good food is and where it is being served. *Petros* and the other Kogeones Brothers decided that in order to succeed, one must serve the best at reasonable prices. In his "Palace," The Dianna's Restaurant "OPAA," *Petros* reigns supreme as host to everybody from the humblest to the most famous celebrity that comes to eat real Greek food as it is supposed to be cooked and served in an atmosphere of congeniality.

I always wanted to meet this fellow *Petros*. His reputation is ahead of him. I finally met him by a mere accident on "The Streets of Athens." We met at the Hotel Grand Bretagne in Constitution Square and talked about everything and nothing. I didn't interview *Petros*. He interviewed me and that is how I got this yarn together. *Petros* is bursting with vigor. He is bursting forth with excitement, agitation. In a simple word he is effervescent. And now he is more so because he is really angry over the Cyprus case. He is not afraid to talk and tell you what a bunch of bastards the Terrible Turks are. And I guess he is right!

The next day we met again. We went to a studio where they gave Petros a screen test. And after the test we stopped at a road side tavern in the area known as "Aghia Paraskevi" to partake something and quench our hunger. This tavern called "Ta Platania" seems to be a family affair. The people there were seated in long tables. Some one was playing the guitar and the rest were singing to the accompaniment of the Sanduri. The Sanduri player was singing in some voice that I could not tell whether it was baritone or basso.

Anyway, it was a bit of everything. Then the guests drank some very fine retsina. *Petros* drank his share of retsina and got into the well known condition of having developed a "kefi." And when a Greek gets to feeling his "kefi" you are in for a treat.

The people in the tavern sang. The Sanduri player played and sang the people's songs. An 82-year old man began dancing in the gravel covered tavern plaza. They all said that the man is terrific having such kefi at 82-years of age, four scores and two years. Then the kefi began boiling inside *Petros*. He got up to dance alone. He did a syrtaki under the applause of the audience. Then he did a Tsamiko. My friends and felow Greeks, *Petros* is some dancer. His six feet two inches body flies in the air when he dances a Greek dance. Then he put a glass of wine on the top of his head and danced with the glass wine staying proudly above his head. Try that trick some time in your spare time and see if you can do it. All you need is a glass, some retsina, real Greek demotic music and the effervescence of *Petros*. I bet you one dollar to a bail of hay that no dancer on the screen can do what *Petros* can do. He is a real palikari. And as he danced he rained dollars on the ground. A couple of kids would pick them up and give them to the Sanduri player. I bet you that the Sanduri player must have made more money from the rain of dollars by *Petros* than the tavern owner. Boy, do I wish I was years younger that I too can dance like *Petros*. About the only thing that I know that we, *Petros* and I, have in common is that he went to my High School Alma Mater, the Central YMCA at 19 South LaSalle Street.

Petros took College lessons at the YMCA also.

Petros is hunk of man, the son of man, Big! His father was known as "Big Nick" migrated to America he helped build the railroads. He went to Salt Lake City as one of the lieutenants of Louis Skliris. Now some of you might not know who Louis Skliris was. I will tell you. According to the Chicago Tribune of those years the early tens of the 20th Century when the Tribune was a liberal daily, Skliris was named editorially as the "*Abdul Hamid of the West.*" Why was Skliris given such "distinction"? I will tell you why! In those days America was bursting from the seams. Horace Greeley kept urging all young men to "Go West Young Man." The Harrimans, the Vanderbilts, the James Hills and many others were building the railroad and wanted to do it with the cheapest labor they could get. Skliris got them for the Railroad Barons. In fact he was so successful at getting foreigners of all nationalities who could not speak a word of English to work for as much as $1.25 a day, live in box cars and live outside of the town. Skliris had lieutenants like "Big Nick." In fact Skliris broke two national railroad strikes with cheap foreign laborers. In spite of the protests. Skliris broke the strike and as the protesters yelled "Down with Skliris," underneath the governor's window, Skliris smiled with Mephistophelian joy as he looked down and saw the sea of the sons of men. . . pleading for a raise from the railroad barons. These were the years when America was "flexing its muscles." I guess that is the story of the building of every Empire. Good old U.S.A. could not be any different.

"Big Nick," Petros father got the patriotic bug. He returned to Greece in 1912 to fight in the Balkan Wars. He fought in the Battle of Kilkis, Lahana and other battles that the Greeks distinguished themselves for valour. Now "Big Nick's" son *Petros* has the same fervor to fight the Terrible Turk. . . Cyprus is his baby. He, like many thousands of Greeks, is working hard to assist the Cypriots to live as free people. *Petros* is in the forefront of the Greek Americans who are united as one in this new struggle for the grandeur of Greece, the people who taught the world how to live and again are called to give what they have for the sake of human decency and honor in spite of U.S. State Department and CIA policy. And *Petros* says. . ." *God Bless America And All The Greeks.*"

(Reprinted by permission from the *Greek Press* of Chicago)

SAY "OPAA" WHEN YOU THINK GREEK FOOD

Besides being celebrities, Barbara Rush, Caesar Romero, Spiro Agnew, Michael Bakalis, Paul Simon, Kup, Len O'Connor, Jimmy the Greek, Elke Summer, and Gene Barry share something else in common.

They've all been to Dianna's "Opaa"—South Halsted Street's newest Greek Restaurant. Owned by Petros Kogiones, Dianna's "Opaa" attracts local personalities as well as visitors from all over the world—as far as Japan, Russia and Saudi Arabia.

Petros, who has a large following from when he ran Dianna's grocery store and restaurant with his brothers gives everybody the VIP treatment. "Dianna's 'Opaa' is the only place where no one is treated as a customer but as a guest," says Petros.

The congenial host also added that he has reversed the adage that the customer is always right. "Petros is always right and knows what is best in Greek cooking and atmosphere for his guests."

Dianna's personifies everything that is Greek. A truly Hellenic setting, the walls carry the message of contemporary Greece. The interior design consists of murals depicting a taverna, shop facades, an outdoor cafe and a peasant's home. Still another mural behind the stage shows Diana the Huntress shooting her bow and arrow. It is after this mythological figure and Petros' native region that he named his restaurant. One of nine children, he comes from Nestani in the southern part of Greece. The mountain overlooking the village is called Artemission—a derivative of Diana.

"Opaa," the second part of the restaurant's name, means "hooray" or an expression of approval. During the Christmas holidays, even Santa in Dianna's changed his "ho-ho-ho" to "opaa."

Petros was an elementary school teacher in Greece before joining his brothers Peter, Ted, George and Demos 11 years ago in Chicago. A bachelor, he works 12 to 16 hours every day tending to every detail—from that special welcome for the ladies to supervising the spotlessly clean kitchen. "When you see people happy at the restaurant, you don't mind the long hours seven days a week. But you must like people and never think in terms of dollars."

Now, everybody say "opaa."

(The West Central Association Bulletin)

This Certifies That

Dianna's Opaa

has been selected for Special Commendation on the WBBM Newsradio 78 *Restaurant Review.*

Honorable Mention

1974

SHERMAN M. KAPLAN
Anchorman/Reporter
Restaurant Critic
WBBM NEWSRADIO 78

WILLIAM C. O'DONNELL
Vice-President CBS Radio Division
General Manager
WBBM NEWSRADIO 78

Petros' *Dianna's Opaa* is world's most honored restaurant. A one-of-a-kind place attracting new and old alike. Once you are introduced to Petros' way of hosting his "cousins" of both sexes you become addicted to *Dianna's Opaa*. And anyone who gets addicted to *Dianna's* will never need any other form of addiction.

Chicago State University

HISTORY DEPARTMENT

Ninety-Fifth Street at King Drive
Chicago, Illinois 60628

OCTOBER 31, 1973

MR. PETROS KOGEONES
DIANNA'S RESTAURANT
212 SO. HALSTED ST.
CHICAGO, ILLINOIS 60607

DEAR PETROS,

    DR. RITA C. KUCERA, STUDENTS AND GUESTS OF CHICAGO STATE UNIVERSITY, AND MYSELF EXPRESS OUR DEEPEST THANKS AND APPRECIATION TO YOU AND THE FINE STAFF OF DIANNA'S FOR A MOST MEMORABLE AND EXCITING EVENING. IT WAS VERY KIND AND GENEROUS OF YOU AND DIANNA'S TO PROVIDE SUCH AN OPPORTUNITY FOR STUDENTS TO DISCOVER (MOST OF THEM FOR THE FIRST TIME) WHAT IT REALLY MEANS TO BE A GREEK. WHILE RITA AND I CAN TEACH THE FACTS, IT WAS YOU, PETROS, WHO GOT OVER TO OUR STUDENTS AND THEIR GUESTS THE MEANING AND SPIRIT.

    SPEAKING PERSONALLY, I STILL RECALL MY FIRST ENCOUNTER WITH GREEK FOOD AND WINE OVER 12 YEARS AGO, WHEN DIANA'S WAS A FEW TABLES BEHIND THE GROCERY STORE. OVER THE PAST DECADE THE KOGEONES BROTHERS HAVE MADE DIANNA'S FOR MYSELF AND FOR MANY OF MY FRIENDS A HOME AWAY FROM HOME, A PLACE OF REFRESHMENT FOR THE HUMAN SPIRIT, AND AT TIMES A REFUGE FROM THE MADNESS OF THE WORLD OUTSIDE. FOR MANY OF US DIANNA'S HAS BECOME GOD'S GIFT TO CHICAGO, AND WE ARE SURE OTHER CITIES ENVY CHICAGO FOR HAVING THE KOGEONES BROTHERS.

    WE WISH FOR YOU, PETROS, FOR YOUR BROTHERS, AND FOR DIANNA'S ENDLESS YEARS OF PROSPERITY AND SUCCESS IN CHICAGO.

SINCERELY "OPAA",

DR. ROBERT J. KOVARIK

I'D RATHER HAVE A COOK

We may live without poetry, music and art;
We may live without conscience and live without heart;
We may live without friends; we may live without books
But civilized man cannot live without cooks.

                        Athenaeus: Deipnosophists

No question about it, the success or failure of a restaurant—any nationality restaurant—depends on the competence of its chef.

Although I am the last to insult a chef of proven ability I must confess I'd rather have a dish from mama's or aunt Sophia's kitchen. Then I know the meal was prepared with loving care and the best of ingredients, because they would not allow anything to get out of their kitchen unless it was perfect.

Unless you make a *tsorba,* a chicken soup from the broth of 60-100 chickens, and this is only made in specializing restaurants in Constantinople, you cannot compare the taste of home-made Greek dishes with the ones prepared in restaurants in large quantities. Even dishes called *tis horas,* made to order, like lamb chops or broiled *tchipoura* are a hundred times tastier if cooked at home. One reason is that the chef has to pay attention to 10, 20 or 50 different meals he is preparing at the same time, while mama consentrates at one. Except if the chef is a fussy genius who refuses to allow anything to get out of his kitchen unless it is A-OK.

Now, if you can get a combination of a home made dish and a first class chef to prepare it for you, then you are in for a great feast, a real *Banquet of the Learned*, a *symposium* as is so masterfully described in the *Deipnosophists* by Athenaeus.

The recipes in this book are for the best home made Greek dishes. If you follow the instructions carefully there is no reason why *you* should not become a first class chef and earn a white *kamilafki.*

If you wonder what on earth a *kamilafki* is, it is the black cap a priest or monk wears in Greece. Cooks who, during the Middle Ages, prepared food in monasteries wore white *kalimafki* to distinguish themselves from the monks. And, during those periods, monks, believe me, knew how to appreciate a succulent dish.

Although I do not claim I can get close to the genius of Thimbron the Athenian who was universally recognized as the greatest cook of all times, I'm sure *you* will become a good enough cook to wear a white *kamilafki* and distinguish yourself for your skill in the kitchen if you follow carefully my recipes.

And do not forget: all the dishes are Greek in spite the turkish names of some of them. You see, following the fall of Constantinople in 1453 the Turks renamed the dishes as everything else in the Greek world. For nearly four centuries Greek cooks were preparing Greek dishes with turkish names. They kept them because it was hard to go back to the ancient language that became along with the latin, obsolete. Yet, if you are an *epicurian*, "one given to the gratification of eating and drinking" as Webster defines the word, do not forget Epicurus was a Greek philosopher and his students were preparing those *lucullian* banquets continuously improving the gastronomical standards since antiquity.

LEARNED MEN AT SUPPER

Give not the sweetbreads of Lybia,
Nor the spicy gravy of Media,
But that simple and tasteless lentil soup
Where my greek poverty meets
All its overflowing luxury.

Author unknown: Deipnosophists

Achilles became immortal by eating *ambrosia*, the God's food and if it wasn't for his weak spot, his heel, he would probably be around to write his own famous recipes—a best seller of all best sellers no doubt.

Zeus, the God of gods, was raised by eating *ambrosia* and drinking *nektar*, according to mythology, but no one can tell for sure what the food and drink of gods consisted of. Most of the learned men of the antiquity agree both *ambrosia* and *nektar* were honey. Whatever it is, one thing is sure. It takes an exceptionally good dish to be called *ambrosia* and it takes the best of wines to justify the name *nektar*. I hope by following my recipes carefully you may be able to serve some day some kind of *ambrosia* to your guest, a masterpiece of yours.

When at supper, learned men of the antiquity devoted a considerable amount of time. It looked like a convention, a gathering of intellectuals to talk informally about all kinds of subjects, without an agenda. They were talking about literature and philosophy, poetry and law, medicine and astronomy and their endless discussions were frequently interrupted by fabulous eating and drinking accompanied by soft music.

Cookery and food—poultry, fish, meat, vegetables and desserts—were extensively discussed and a celebrated compilation of their discussions has come down to us by Athenaeus, an Egyptian of Greek ancestry of the 3d century A.D., who wrote no less than 30 books under the general title of *Deipnosophists—or Learned Men At Supper* to describe in detail some of the convivial qualities of the ancient Greeks.

Famous were, of course, their *symposia* or banquets which were frequent because, as Athenaeus tells us, "friendly comrades should not abstain too long from having a symposium, since it is the most delightful way to remember each other."

An idea of what an original Homeric banquet consisted of, we get from Athenaeus:

"The house master places polished tables before his guests and breaks the bread, whereas the carcer brings platters of meat, roasted meat, mostly beef, by which the body and the soul may enjoy strength. Never does he place before them elaborate and complicated dishes, requiring the complex tricks of the culinary art, nor does he serve to them energizing appetizers, rare birds, nightingales, tongues, aphrodisic drinks and any such dainties, as those suffocating the dining tables of the barbarians—all of them marks of luxury which awakened riotous desires."

This encomium to simplicity Athenaeus wrote to emphasize the difference between Greek and barbarian cookery.

"When the queen of Carians, in Asia Minor, made it a point to send Alexander the Great fancy dishes and sweetmeats, prepared in unusual ways by the hands of famous chefs and noted artists, he wrote her a letter of thanks adding he could not eat any of these exotic dishes since he had better and fancier cooks serving to him night marches for breakfast and frugal breakfast for dinner."

Ancient Greeks indeed had a bitter experience of barbarian dinners. When the persian king Xerxes, leading his mighty army to Greece, stopped in the island of Thassos for lunch, the poor Thasians had to sell their houses to secure such luxuries as carpets, golden tables and solid gold plates and cups carried away by the king's retenue after the lunch.

Soon after his departure the Thasians offered thankful sacrifices to gods because Xerxes did not stay for dinner!

The eating habits of the ancient Greeks, form one of the most precious traditions and were preserved to this day through their religious customs.

Let's take a good look at them.

EATING BY THE CALENDAR

To say the Greeks are eating by the calendar is not an exaggeration. What we call Greek civilization is simply a way of life marked by customs and traditions. Eating is an important part in Greek—as in every country's—life. Food and drink follows the day's toil and, as Hesiod the author of the book on the making of the world says, it is a noble claim to have a little *glendi*, a small feast, after the day's work. But not too much.

"*Pan metron ariston*," the ancient Greeks proclaimed. "*Every moderation excellent.*"

To put *glendi* under control and regulate moderation, the Greeks used the calendar. And the Bible. Eating—and drinking for that matter—is guided by the religious festivities—not all of them joyous occasions. All out *glendi* to celebrate New Year, the *Apokria* (Mardi-Gras) and Easter are followed by long periods of lent and Holy Week fasting when every Greek abstains from protein food while Greek home-makers are getting ready for the next joyous occasion.

The *vasilopitta*, St. Basil's cake, should be prepared for New Year, the *mageritsa* together with the Easter eggs for Easter, the *kourabiedes* and *melomakarona* sweets for many other happy occasions.

Actually every period of penitence in the Greek calendar precedes or follows a period of *glendi*. The *Apokria* is followed by the *Sarakosti*, a 40-day period of fasting which precedes the Easter celebrations when lamb in the skewer plays a dominant role.

Christmas and New Year also follow a short period of fasting and every Greek should abstain from protein food at least once a year to receive Holy Communion. There are many occasions of fasting of feasting in the Greek calendar. The *Ipapanti* or Candlemas, an Hebrew religious day (February 2nd) and the Pentecost. The Annunciation and Assumption of the Virgin Mary day. And the *Kathari Deftera*, Monday after the last Sunday of *Apokria* when the entire population of Greece goes to the fields to celebrate *Koulouma* the opening of the 40-day period of fasting until Easter.

While almost every home determines its own periods of fasting the dishes during these periods are practically the same throughout Greece. And the long tradition of fine cooking is still maintained in every Greek home, the only place the casual visitor can appreciate a full range of excellent and truly Greek dishes, the only place authentic Greek cookery can be found. Of course, there are many cooks good in knowledge and enthusiasm in practically every other taverna and good restaurant in Greece. But their menues, as of necessity, must include a continental cuisine and, therefore, only the classic and traditional Greek dishes are included. Many such tavernas as a matter of fact specialize in one or two truly Greek dishes. My recipes are a selection of the best as tested and perfected and acclaimed by thousands and thousands at *Dianna's Opaa*. They also include many of the most valuable secrets of Greek cooking, unpublished and preserved only among friends in Greek homes well-known for a lady excelling in the art of Greek cookery. These ladies love to cook and they make it a point to teach their daughters and—why not? —their sons, the love of food and cooking. When you live high up in the mountains or down in the ports and the islands, cooking becomes a hereditary occupation and the gastronomic heroes in every area are widely acclaimed, like Olympic winners.

I hope, with a little enthusiasm and much love, you will also become a candidate for an Olympic gold medal in Greek Cooking.

Just follow me...

PART II: *KALI OREXI*

"After the toil of the day is over, should you desire be to eat your food in peace and drink a glass of wine to settle yourselves, it is a worthy ambition"

Hesiod

AN ESSAY ON *MEZE*

Appetizers and hors d'oeuvre to the Greek are the all important *meze*. No Greek taverna goes without a variety of *meze*, because taverna customers want to drink wine, *retsina* and *kokineli*—a lot of it. And you must have solid food, a little of everything, to drink. Especially those who like a stronger aperitif, *ouzo*, would not touch it without some *meze*, even if it is only a few olives, slides of cucumber, preferably pickled in vinegar, and small pieces of bread and cheese.

However the variety of Greek *meze* is unlimited and practically every other taverna or even home has its own specialties—and is proud of them. I would suggest that you should specialize in a few *meze* and avoid a great variety, especially of those that are rather hard to prepare in a moment's notice or belong to the same family like *burekakia* which is a general term for small pies in folded or rolled *filo* with a variety of fillings, *feta* with or without spinach, or meat, chicken, and what not.

Actually most of the *meze* are nothing else but very small portions or miniatures of regular dishes and the recipes are incorporated in the original dishes, as *keftedakia* in *keftedes*, *dolmadakia* in *dolmades* etc. Other families of *meze* are found in the salad, fish and vegetable chapters of the book.

In preparing *mezedakia* for your hosts for the evening, always keep in mind in your list to include at least two items to be prepared and served hot in addition to the cold ones.

Flaming Cheese / Saganaki

1 piece of cheese cut in a triangle ("Kasseri" or Kefalotire")	1 egg
1/2 lemon	1 whiskey glass of "Metaxa" or another brandy

Dip cheese into beaten egg, flour it, and then fry it in an oiled or buttered frying pan, turning it over two times. Have a hot pan ready and put the cheese in it. Then pour the "Metaxa" or other brandy on the cheese, light it with a match and say "opaa." Extinguish the flames by squeezing the lemon over the pan. (Serves One).

Cheese Triangles / Tiropitakia

1 (8-ounce) tub dry cottage cheese	1/4 teaspoon garlic powder
1 (4-ounce) package blue cheese	Dab nutmeg
2 (3-ounce) packages cream cheese	1 pound strudel leaves (filo)
1/2 pound imported feta cheese	1 whole egg plus 1 yolk
1/4 pound imported roquefort	1 teaspoon farina
	Melted butter

Blend cheeses and mix thoroghly. Add eggs, garlic powder, farina and nutmeg. Mix well.

Cut filo into strips about 2 inches wide, line them up on a board and brush with melted butter. Place 1 teaspoon of filling on one end of pastry and fold corner over to form a triangle. Continue folding from side to side, in the form of a triangle, until desired size. Line the triangles up in a buttered baking pan and bake in a 375-degree oven until golden brown. Serve hot.

This is Dr. Constantine Tatooles famous "old family" recipe as printed in the Sun-Times, Nov. 8, 1974. We highly recommend it.

Meat Balls / Keftedes

2 lb. minced meat
1 cup of bread crumbs
2 tablespoons olive oil
2 tablespoons grated onion
1 tablespoon vinegar
1 tablespoon chopped mint

1/2 teaspoon oregano
2 cloves garlic (optional)
2 tablespoons boiling water
Salt and pepper
1 tablespoon chopped parsley

Using your hands mix well in a bowl the meat, onions and breadcrumbs. Add the eggs and continue to work the mixture until is well combined. Next mix in the herbs, garlic and olive oil and moisten with vinegar and hot water. Add the seasoning and leave for about one hour before cooking. Shape the mixture in the desired size and flour lightly. Fry in very hot olive oil until well browned. Drain and serve hot.

Keftedes go well with boiled vegetables or salad and you can dip them in hot tomato sauce. For *keftedakia* appetizer simply make them in smaller size.

You can also make baked keftedes cooking slowly for 1 1/2 hours in moderate oven. Add a cup of milk, a cup of tomato juice and a tin of tomatoes.

Stuffed Vine Leaves / Dolmades

25 vine leaves (young and tender)
1 teaspoon chopped mint
1 teaspoon dill
Bunch of spring onions

4 oz. rice
1/2 pint olive oil
1/2 pint boiling water
Salt and pepper

This recipe is for meatless *dolmades*. To make *dolmadakia* appetizers simply make the dolmades as tiny as possible.

When using fresh vine leaves blanch them in boiling water, drain and cool them. Cook the rice in the boiling water for 5 minutes. Mix the rice well with the onions and seasoning and the olive oil and cook over low flame for 10 minutes stirring the mixture from time to time.

Use a tablespoon of the mixture on each leaf at the stem end. Roll tightly. Place them on a pan, layer on layer, and add some water. Cover them to prevent breaking and cook slowly. Simmer for about one hour. You can serve with yoghourt on top, or egg and lemon sauce.

If you like you can add finely minced meat in your mixture and you can use cabbage instead of vine leaves.

Spinach Pie / Spanakopitta

3 pounds fresh spinach
2 bunches green scallions, finely chopped
1/2 cup minced parsley
1 pound crumbled feta cheese
1/2 pound filo pastry leaves
1/2 teaspoon dill (optional)
8 eggs, beaten
olive oil
1 cup melted butter
salt

Wash the spinach, cut off the stems, dry completely with towels, and chop. Brown the scallions in 1/2 cup olive oil until tender. Combine spinach, parsley, dill, beaten eggs and cheese; add cooked scallions; season with salt lightly and mix well. Grease a 9X13-inch baking pan and line with 5 of the filo sheets, brushing each sheet with the melted butter combined with 1/2 cup olive oil. Spread the spinach mixture over the filo, and top with remaining sheets of filo, brushing each again with the butter and oil. Brush the top sheet, and bake at 350 digrees for 45 minutes. Cool and cut into squares (for best results cut through the filo with a razor blade). This may be served hot or cold, as an appetizer in small squares, as a vegetable side-dish in larger squares, or even after meals with a chilled white retsina.

To make spinach triangles prepare the filling as explained for spinach pie. Place a teaspoonful of the filling on the filo leaves and proceed to fold, brush with butter and bake in the same manned as cheese triangles.

Varieties

Every Greek taverna, restaurant or home likes to make its own variety of *mezedakia*. Improvision is highly appreciated by Greek gourmands. Olives, feta cheese, cucumbers, tomatoes, and pickled peppers are always a must among Greek appetizers. Greek tavernas by the sea will serve fresh clams, delicious fried *marides* (smelts), *kalamarakia* (baby squid), *garides* (shrimps) or boiled octopus with lots of vinegar. Even the simplest wayside tavernas will serve you *melitzanosalata* (egg plant salad) or *taramosalata* (fish roe salad) or *glykadakia* (sweetbreads) etc., etc. Recipes are to be found in the appropriate chapters of this book.

All dressed up in national costume for Greek Independence Day at the *Paidagogiki Academy* of Tripolis

Dancing the *tsamiko* at *Dianna's Opaa*

← High Kicking Greek dance with National Guard Evzones in Chicago for the annual parade.

← Teaching some of the thousands of beauties the *syrtaki*

🔺 Reminiscing the fantastic times in Greece with Richard Egan of "The 300 Spartans" motion picture fame

🔺 Jim Londos, of world wrestling champion fame is hosted by Petros after leading the Greek Independence Day parade as Grand Marshall

🔻 Bill Kurtis, CBS newscaster has a toast of brandy with Petros

An anonymous artist fell in love with Petros and this is what her talent produced

With Irv Kupcinet, the No 1 TV interviewer and newspaper columnist in the country

Flowers, Grecian beauties and Petros adorn *Dianna's Opaa* float in the Greek Independence Day parade in Chicago

Nickolaos Kogiones, a hero of the 1912-13 Balkan Wars is Petros' father

Leading the *Kalamatiano* with his brother Peter and the Kontessa

← Prince Petros of Greece and Denmark meets Petros of Nestani and Chicago for a royal dinner at *Dianna's Opaa*

← Governor Walker of Illinois, a regular at *Dianna's Opaa,* enjoys getting some inside information from Petros

◆ Lovely movie star Elke Sommer always has a grand time with Petros and his *Saganaki*

◆ When Greek meets Greek it spells *glendi* and good time and movie star George Maharis enjoys it immensely

◆ High caliber newspaperwomen are Petros' favorites and so is Mary Daniels feature writer and columnist of Chicago Tribune and Georgie Anne Geyer staff writer of the Chicago Daily News

⬆ The entire cast of the world-renown serial "Hogan's Heroes" had the time of their lives at *Dianna's Opaa* with Petros' specialties

⬇ Caesar Romero (no other introduction needed) learns a few points in Greek dancing from Petros, after a fabulous dinner at *Dianna's Opaa*

ADVENTURE IN HERBS

Hardly any Greek cookery goes without herbs. Not knowing them thouroughly makes you look like an amateur lightweight trying to step into a ring with a heavyweight champion.

However, for our purposes, and not to confuse you with many Greek herbs, rarely used for culinary purposes, we confined in the "big ten"—those used in everyday dishes. We suggest that you always keep some of these—either fresh in your refrigirator, or dry in your kitchen cabinets.

Here they are:

Oregano / *Rigani*
Parsley / *Maidano*
Bay / *Dafni*
Dill / *Anitho*
Celery / *Selino*

Mint / *Diosmos*
Rosemary / *Dendrolivano*
Marjoram / *Mantzourana*
Capers / *Kapari*
Cumin / *Kimino*

Of secondary importance are the basil (*vasilikos*) confined in Greek cooking to the flavouring of preserves, thyme (*thymari*) used with oil to preserve olives, sage (*fascomilo*), chamomile and lime flowers (*tilio*) used for sore throats and coughs. Other herbs are rather used in medicine and their knowledge may have wondrous therapeutic effects for the body. I could write another book on them.

Coming back to the "big ten" I would say *oregano* is the most extensively used by Greek cooks. It gives flavor to a tomato salad as well as a fried lamb chop or a grilled fish. But you should be careful with it as with every other herb. Do not overdo it because you may destroy the taste of any dish.

Some may argue that *selino* is not really a herb and I think it is besides the point. The point is that you should always have some crunch, crisp celery sticks available in your refrigerator. The leaves are widely used by Greek cooks for flavouring and if you like boiled fish and a good *psarosoupa*, you cannot have it without celery. *Selino* is also used, with carrots and other vegetables, to decorate fish dishes before serving.

Fresh *maidano* is the next widely used herb. The best way to use it is fresh and chopped. Practically every other Greek dish requires parsley for flavour. *Diosmos* also gives a nice mint flavor as is *daphni* which can be found dry in a grocery. Greek women in the villages boil branches of bay and use the water to rinse table and even bed linen. It gives them a delicious aroma.

Kimino is only used in *stifado* and *sudjukakia*, while *dendrolivano* goes well under the skin of lamb before roasting, but it should be used sparingly and just a spring of it.

Anitho, to the contrary, is used very widely for most meat, fish and even vegetable dishes but it should be bought fresh and kept in the refrigerator along with *maidano* and *selino*.

Some Greek women substitute *rigani* with *mantzourana* to give sweetness to the dish, but this is one herb you may forget about if you do not have it available.

Last, but not least, *capari* is a must to every Greek home. It is usually pickled in wine vinegar and used to garnish all boiled and even broiled fish dishes. It also complements the *horiatiki* salad.

THE NOTORIOUS *SALTSADES*

Greeks are notorious *saltsades*. They love to dip their bread in anything liquid. In coffee, wine or even plain drinking water. But, mostly, they love to dip it in a delicious sauce or dressing. A good *saltsas* is one who loves and appreciates good sauce.

While in the food super markets there is now available a very wide variety of ready-made sauces and dressings of practically every other nationality, French, Italian, Russian or even Hungarian, the Greek sauce and dressing cannot become institutionalized because of its variety. In every Greek kitchen you can find a repertoire of sauces and dressings quite different from the house next door. Here, again is an area that you can improvise playing—carefully—with herbs. Once you have acquired a mastery of the taste of herbs, and in this you can only succeed by trial and error, you'll be able to prepare the most delicious sauces and dressings in a jiffy.

To begin with, you only need to learn the basic sauces and dressings in Greek cooking, and here they are:

Olive Oil And Vinegar / Ladoxido

Basic for uncooked salads. Use equal amounts of oil and vinegar, a teaspoon of each is enough for a family salad, and salt and pepper to taste and mix using a spoon before you pour over the salad. It is better to do the mixing in the salad bowl and then toss in the lettuce and turn them over with a wooden spoon until all of them are coated and no liquid is left in the bowl.

Olive Oil And Lemon / Ladolemono

Greeks are using lemon instead of vinegar in boiled cabbages, green vegetables and summer salads. The difference here is in posology. Use three parts olive oil and one part lemon. There is also a difference between *ladolemono* dressing and *ladolemono* sauce, served with boiled or grilled fish, lobster and mostly used as a substitute to mayonnaise.

To make it use 1/2 cup of olive oil and two tablespoons of lemon juice and beat them until thoroghly combined. Then add a tablespoon of chopped parsley, salt and pepper and serve. You must make this sauce just before serving because olive oil and lemon will separate soon after beating.

Egg Lemon / Avgolemono

3 egg yolks (or 3 whole eggs) 4 tablespoons lemon juice
2-3 tablespoons hot broth

Avgolemono claims the title of national sauce of Greece. It goes to many dishes and goes well, especially if the dish has some liquid from which to take 2 or 3 tablespoons and add them to the sauce as you work.

You beat the yolks first, fluffy and light. Then you add the lemon juice, and gradually the liquid from the dish you have prepared. Beat until the sauce has a unified color and then stir it into the dish you are making. Cover the pan and leave it about 5 minutes on the side of the stove. Do not allow the sauce to boil.

White / Bechamel

      2 ounces flour   1 1/2 pint milk
      2 ounces butter   Salt, pepper, nutmeg

Work the flour as you heat the butter in a saucepan. Add milk gradually. Stir continuously. Cook in slow fire for about 20 minutes—until the flour is smooth and odorless. Add salt, pepper and nutmeg while stirring.
You can add eggs and cheese if you like.
This sauce called bechamel is basic and, therefore, mentioned in many dishes.

Tomato Sauce / Saltsa Tomata

This is the same Italians use to serve with macaroni: The Greeks serve it also with rice. Although one can classify the tomato sauce as Greco-Roman, especially in view of the fact that Greeks, like Italians, serve tomato meat sauce, *domata saltsa me kima,* the Greek way is somehow differerent:

    2 pouunds tomatoes (ripe)   1 dessertspoon sugar
    2 ounces butter   1 stick cinnamon
    1 medium size onion   1 bay leaf
    1 glass of red wine   1 sprig basil
    1/2 cup of water   Salt and pepper

Make the tomatoes mashed after you skin them and take the seeds out. In a pan, melt the butter and add the tomatoes with the onion, herbs and seasoning. Cook for 15 minutes and then add water and the wine. Lower the flame to simmer for another 30 minutes until the sauce has slightly thickened. You should remove the cinnamon stick, bay leaf and basil before serving.
When making the tomato sauce with meat add a pound of finely minced veal to the above ingredients. The meat, *kima,* should be cooked first for fifteen minutes in low fire before putting the tomatoes etc. Also when melting the butter add the onion and a little water. Final cooking should be extended to about one hour.
Greeks also like to make tomato sauce with liver instead of minced veal. To make it richer, many add a small glass of vermouth or cooking brandy just before taking out of the fire the sauce.

Mayonnaise / Mayoneza

2 eggs (yolk)	1/2 teaspoon dry mustard
3 cups olive oil	1/2 teaspoon sugar
3 tablespoons lemon juice	Salt and pepper

By taking a glance at the ingredients you may understand why Greek *mayoneza* has nothing in common with the ready-made mayonnaise of the food supermarkets. Greeks use a smooth bowl and a wooden spoon and apply a slow and steady stirring to achieve a high quality home made mayonnaise. First, you put the salt, pepper, mustard and sugar in the bowl and stir strongly and evenly for a few minutes after you break in the yolk of eggs. As you stir add one cup of olive oil drop by drop. Then alternate, adding a little lemon juice and the remaining olive oil as you proceed in stirring making sure you keep a consistency until desired flavour is reached. Should the *mayoneza* curdle do not despair. Break the yolk of another egg in a clean bowl and work by adding gradually the curdled mayonnaise. The main difference between *mayoneza* and ready-made mayonnaise is that the Greeks use lemon juice instead of vinegar and have established their posology, a proportion of olive oil, lemon juice and egg yolk to obtain a jelly-like consistency.

Garlic Sauce / Skordalia

6 medium size potatoes or	Juice of 2 lemons
2 cups of bread crumbs	3/4 cup olive oil
6-8 cloves garlic	1 teaspoon salt

If you love to pound in a mortar you are going to like making *skordalia*—odor and all. The potatoes must be boiled and peeled and cooled first. In the meantime you crush the garlic adding salt. If you make it with crumbs crash them together and add the olive oil and lemon juice gradually. Alternate oil and lemon drop by drop until you have thick cream, the same as mayonnaise.

LOVE OF SALADS

Unless you mess things up and Greeks accuse you of turning them into a *salata*, the word mean salad. Greeks mess a lot of things and also make a lot of salads. They love their *salata* as much as *a saltsa* and they have a way of turning almost any dish into a *salata* one. There is hardly a vegetable it cannot be prepared as a salad, green or cooked. It is a very useful addition to a cold buffet and can be served as an appetizer. Even a roast lamb by adding some olive oil and vinegar can be turned into a *salata*.

It takes only a minute to a Greek housewife to slice some lettuce and green pepper into thin strips, cut up two or three tomatoes to pieces the size of walnut and mix them in a salad bowl with a dozen or so of Kalamata olives and a few ounces of *feta* cheese cut into small cubes. Pouring some olive oil and wine vinegar and seasoning with salt and pepper and turning the whole thing several times with wooden fork and spoon makes the standard mixed Greek salad.

Additions and variations are infinite and it is up to you to improvise with the help of spring onions, chopped dill or fennel, capers, sliced pickles, oregano, etc., etc.

A very popular variation of the mixed *salata* is the *horiatiki*.

Mixed / Horiatiki

Assorted greens (lettuce, chicory, watercress)
Tomatoes, chilled, peeled and quartered
Cucumbers, peeled and sliced
Green onions, thinly sliced
Anchovies
Greek olives
Capers
Radishes
Feta cheese
Vinegar, olive oil and oregano

This is the classic Greek salad. Wash, dry and chop the greens. If you have a large wooden platter rub it with garlic. Arrange the greens in the center, cover with rows of sliced cucumbers, sprinkle with chopped onions and capers, surround them with sliced radishes and and encircle the eldge of the platter with tomato wedges and anchovy strips intermingled. Garnish with olives. Sprinkle with oregano, oil and vinegar. Add feta cheese cubes all over the salad.

Eggplant Salad / Melitzanosalata

1 large or 2 medium eggplant
1 garlic clove
1 onion
1 tablespoon parsley
1 large tomato
1 teaspoon marjoram
1 teaspoon fine herbs
olive oil

Bake the eggplant for one hour after you pierce it with a fork several times. Peel and chop the eggplant. Add garlic mashed, and the onion grated, the tomato peeled and chopped, parsley, herbs and enough olive oil to moisten the mixture. Mix well and chill. *Melitzanosalata* may be served as a dip or *meze*, with crackers, tomato wedges and Greek olives, or on a bed of lettuce.

Fish Roe Salad / Taramosalata

6 ounces t a r a m a (1 jar)　　1/4 pound bread slices
3 spring onions　　2 cups olive oil
3 lemons　　1 teaspoon chopped dill

Dip the *tarama* in water to remove some of the salt. After a few minutes put it in a mortar and with a pestle squeeze out any excessive water. Work slowly, the same way as in preparing mayonnaise, by adding olive oil drop by drop and squeezing the juice of the lemons. Have the spring onions finely sliced and mix them together with the chopped dill and the bread slices, trimmed. For better taste use rye bread. Work steadily until you obtain an evenly looking mixture. *Taramosalata* should be pink in color and fluffy enough to be used as a dip. A variation is the use of boiled potato instead of bread or both. When serving garnish with Kalamata olives.

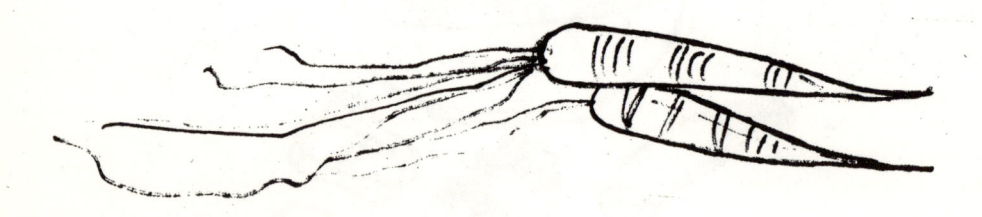

Yoghourt Salad / Tzatziki

1 pound yoghourt　　1 tablespoon vinegar
1 cucumber　　3 cloves garlic
1 tablespoon olive oil　　Salt

This is an excellent dip especially for summer parties. Peel the cucumber and cut it into tiny cubes. Slice the garlic cloves finely. Add salt to taste and beat the mixture for awhile. Chill and serve very cold. You can garnish with paprika or use chopped mint instead of garlic. Macedonians use this as a must *meze* for their *ouzo* apperitif. It is a very welcome addition during summertime picnics.

Potato Salad / Patatosalata

2 pounds small potatoes
1 onion
2 tablespoons olive oil
1 dessertspoon wine vinegar
Parsley, salt and pepper

Boil the potatoes in their skins and watch them not to split by over-boiling. After they are cool enough to handle them remove the skin and cut them into small cubes. Add the onion finely sliced and a good handfull of chopped parsley. Pour over a dressing of olive oil, vinegar, salt and pepper when they are still relatively warm, but serve cold. *Patatosolata* goes well with fried or broiled fish.

Bean Salad / Fassolia Salata

Fassolia salata are prepared the same way as *patatosalata*. The beans should be cooked tender in plenty of boiling salted water. Leave them to cool after you drain them and then dress them up with olive oil and lemon juice or wine vinegar. Serve cold. This salad goes also well with fried fish or grilled meats.

Boiled Vegetables Salad / Horta Salata

Most of the vegetables, and especially *radikia* (dandelion), *padzaria* (beets), *lahano* (cabbage), *kunupidi* (cauliflower), *spanaki* (spinach), *kolokithakia* (squash), *vrouves* (charlock), are prepared and served as a salad, after boiling. However, since they also make a welcomed side dish to many fish and meat dishes, they are included in the vegetables chapter.

SPEAKING OF SOUPS

The Greeks are traditionally a *litodiaitos* (temperate in their diet) people. Some *feta* cheese with olive oil, bread and an onion are enough for their lunch and even dinner — with a quarter of *retsina* wine, of course.

However, they appreciate a good soup to dip their bread and because this luxury was considered dangerous for the eagerness of the Spartan youth, Lycurgus, the founder and dictator of Sparta allowed only the "black broth" — a horrible tasting soup made of pork, blood and vinegar.
In ancient Athens, to the contrary, soup was a "royal" dish in the best households. It seems that opposite the royal-lentil soup the "democratic" *fassolada,* the bean soup is the most popular.

There are countless varieties of soups in the Greek list including the festive *mageritsa,* a classic post-midnight dish to celebrate Easter. The *kakavia,* counterpart of the French *bouillabaisse* fish soup and the *patsa* (tripe) are the favored dishes of fishermen in the numerous Greek islands. And, last, but not least the *avgolemono* soup is a must in the menu of of every Greek restaurant.

Egg And Lemon Soup / Avgolemono

3 cups chicken broth
1 cup of rice
3 eggs
2 lemons' juice
Salt and
pepper

This is the most popular and easiest of Greek soups. Bring chicken broth to a boil, salt to taste, add rice, simmer, covered, for 20 minutes; and then remove from fire. In a bowl, beat egg whites until stiff; add yolks and beat well; slowly add lemon juice to eggs, and beat continuously; then add 2 cups of the hot chicken broth and not stop beating. When the eggs and broth are well mixed, pour this mixture back into the remaining broth and rice. Stil well over heat. Care must be taken not to let the soup boil once the eggs and lemon juice have been added. This to prevent curdling.
You can use vermicelli, tapioka, or any of the many soup macaronis. If you desire a cream soup thicken the broth with a little flour before adding the rice. Serve immediately.

Bean Soup / Fassolada

1 1/2 pound lentils
2 large onions chopped
3 celery branches chopped
2 small carrots chopped
3 clover garlic sliced
3 bay leaves
4 tablespoons
olive oil
2 dessertspoons wine
vinegar
1 dessertspoon flour
Salt and pepper

This is another traditional dish of the Greeks. With olives, bread and retsina constitutes an entire dinner — especially during winter months.
The beans must be soaked in water overnight and after a thorough rinse in the morning, put into a pan with enough fresh water to cover them and brought quickly to a boiling point. Then let them simmer for five minutes and drain the water.
Have enough hot water to cover them after you add the onion, carrots, celery leaves and olive oil and season them as desired.
The beans should be cooked slowly for about 1 1/2 hour. If necessary you add more water from time to time.
The tomatoes are optional. If used should be added last, about 45 minutes before serving. If not in a can they must be skinned and pulped. If you do not use tomatoes add lemon juice.

Lentil Soup / Faki

1 1/2 pound white beans
3 carrots finely cubed
1 large onion finely slashed
3 tablespoon celery leaves
finely chopped

4 ripe tomatoes or
an 8-ounce tomato sauce can
1/2 cup olive oil
Salt and
pepper

Lentils do not necessarily have to be soaked in water overnight. Wash them well and boil them covered with cold water in a pan. Have the onions, garlic, bay leaves and olive oil ready and after you drain off the water add them and cover them with fresh water. Bring to the boiling point again and then simmer gently until the lentils are soft. It takes about an hour, depending on the freshness of the lentils. The vinegar, mixed well with the flour, should be added last with seasoning. You may add 2 tablespoons of tomato paste if you like. Then you cook for 10 more minutes.

Lentil soup is a basic dish for the period of Lent, as its name indicates.

Chicken Soup / Kotosoupa

1 boiling chicken
3 eggs
2 lemons

1/2 cup rice
1 small onion
Celery, salt and pepper

Insert half of the onion into the chicken and cover it with water in a pan, adding the other half of the onion, celery, and seasoning. Simmer slowly for about two hours after you bring the water to boiling. Take the chicken out when it is well cooked. Strain the broth and pour it back to the pan to reheat. Add the rice when the broth is bubbling and cook for about fifteen minutes. Beat the eggs with the lemons juice adding two tablespoons of cold water. When the mixture is foamy add some broth and continue beating and adding a little broth at a time. Then pour it all in the pan and stir gently. Do not let the soup boil because it will curdle. You may eliminate the rice and substitute with two tablespoons of flour to make a creamy soup. The difference between the *avgolemono* soup and the *kotosoupa* is obvious. You boil the chicken with half onion inserted and some more added, with celery.

Tomato Soup / Tomatosoupa

2 pounds ripe tomatoes	1 tablespoon
1 potato	tomato paste
1 onion	1 teaspoon sugar
2 tablespoons olive oil	Parsley, celery,
(or butter)	salt and pepper

All the vegetables should be put together in a pan with six cups of water. Chop the vegetables rather coarsly and bring to boil. After adding the olive oil and butter with sugar and seasoning. Let simmer until soft. Pass the broth through a fine sieve and put it back in the pan to boil once again. Add the tomato paste when bubbling and simmer for about ten more minutes. Careful! The parsley should be chopped and added as a garnish before serving.

Vermicelli Soup / Fides

4 pounds vermicelli	Lemon juice
2 ounces butter	and salt

This is a very light soup Greeks serve to recovering patients. The vermicelli is boiled in salted water and should be cooked quickly until boiling. Add the butter with sugar and seasoning. Let simmer until soft. Pass the broth through A variation of this soup is by using meat or poultry broth instead of plain water. In such case eliminate the butter. This is a very nourishing soup made easily and rapidly.

Yellow Lentil Soup / Fava

1 1/2 pound yellow lentils	1/2 cup olive oil
2 onions	Salt

Fava is a favorite soup in the Greek islands. In the mainland, few restaurants and small tavernas include it in their menu. Households have almost abandoned this soup. Actually one can argue if *fava* is really a soup or a vegetable dish, like mashed potato. The yellow lentil soup, inspite of its pure type of dish, is a soup more than anything else. Let's say *fava* is a soup you can eat with a fork, and let it stand at that.

The yellow lentils should be washed and cleaned thoroughly by removing all foreign substances and uneven ones. Any scum that rises to the surface while you boil them in water should be removed. Add the olive oil and onions, finely chopped when the soup comes to the boiling point. Let it simmer for about 1 1/2 hour until the lentils become soft. Then add salt and pass through a sieve. When cool, it should be thick like mashed potato. The best gravy for *fava* is plenty of olive oil and lemon juice. Garnish with finely sliced onion and Kalamata olives.

Chick-Pea Soup / Revithia

1 1/2 pound chick-peas	1 dessertspoon
2 onions	baking soda
1/2 cup olive oil	Salt and pepper

Like *fava*, *revithia* is a winter dish mostly made in small restaurants and tavernas in Greece, just to warm up and fill the stomach. The chick-peas should be soaked overnight in salted cold water. Drain the water in the morning and throw the chick-peas in a large kitchen napkin or white cloth and rub them by adding the soda until their skin is removed. Clean them well, put them in a pan, cover with water and, while boiling, remove the scum as it rises to the surface to keep the water clear. Add the onions, sliced finely, the olive oil, and a sprinkle of pepper. Simmer for about two hours until soft. Wine vinegar or lemon juice go equally well with *revithia*. Add when serving.

Fish Soup / Psarosoupa

Almost any large size fish is good to boil and make a broth out of it. Usually this soup is prepared like the *avgolemono* soup with the same ingredients. You can substitute the *avgolemono* with tomato. In such a case add 1 1/2 pounds of ripe peeled and chopped tomatoes and a tablespoon of tomato paste with 2 tablespoons of olive oil to the fish broth, season with salt and pepper and simmer for half an hour. Then add half a cup of rice and boil quickly until soft. Some lemon juice should be squeezed before serving. You may also sprinkle it with chopped parsley. There are many variations of *psarosoupa*. In the Greek islands, fishermen nearly always use for their soups small fish, after they select the large one for the market and they have plenty of tiny ones of many varieties, very hard to sell, as leftovers. This makes the delicious *kakavia* soup, also known as *bouillabaissse*.

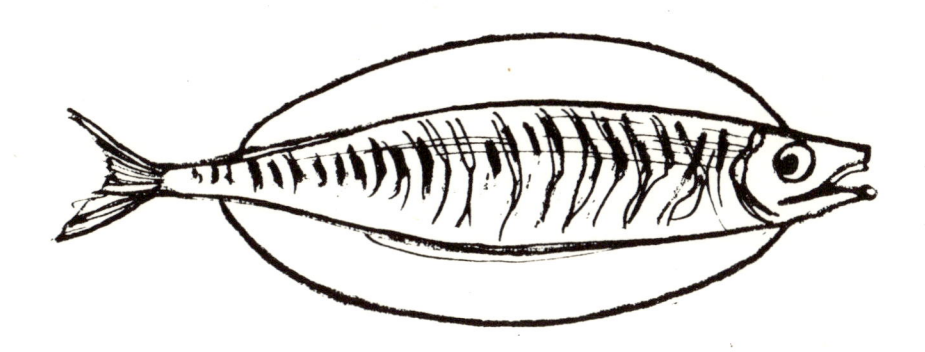

Bouillabaisse / Kakavia

2-3 pounds small fish, shrimp and octopus	1 pound ripe tomatoes
2 medium size onions	2 lemons
2 potatoes	1/2 cup olive oil
	Celery, salt and pepper

French from Marseilles made this fish soup known the world over and there are many different ways to make it. But Phocaean Greeks who had the port of Marseilles as the most important in northern Mediterranean were the ones who introduced the recipe. In fact *bouillabaisse* and *kakavia* have the same connotation meaning a pot (*bouillote* and *katsarola*). A large pot is your tool and you should use enough water. Boil with the onions, potatoes and tomatoes sliced roughly and add the oil and seasoning. After boiling for about half an hour you should have the fish ready, cut in two or three. Throw them in the pot and make sure there is enough water to cover them. Boil for another 15-20 minutes with the pot open, until the flesh of the fish separates from the bones. Add lemon juice and serve with croutons if desired.

Tripe Soup / Patsas

3 pounds tripe
1 medium size onion
3 eggs
2 lemons' juice
Salt

If you don't mind the odor *patsas* is one of the tastier if not the tastiest Greek soup. Just make sure the tripe is washed, and washed and washed before you put it into boiling salted water and let it simmer for about 10 minutes in the pan. Scum will rise to the top and you should remove it with a large spoon. Add the whole onion, cover and press the tripe to the bottom of the pan using a pyrolex plate and cook gently until it becomes tender. Then take it from the broth and let it cool. You cut it into small pieces and put it back into the same water. Beat the eggs with the lemon juice and mix gradually with the broth. You can use a little flour to thicken the broth if too thin. Cook for another 10 minutes and serve. Delicious.
You can also use lamb or pork feet or cowheel to make patsa, either together or separately.

Easter Soup / Mayeritsa

Heart, liver, lungs and intestines of a young lamb
3 ounces butter
12 spring onions
3 ounces rice
3 eggs
2 lemons' juice
Dill, fennel and mint
(Small bunches)
Salt and pepper

This traditional for after midnight Easter soup is unique in flavor and richness but requires a very special attention.
The intestines should be cleaned and washed carefully inside out. Greek women use a thin stick for the purpose. They rub it between the hands with coarse salt and then rinse thoroughly. Heart, liver and lungs also should be cleaned and washed. Put them all in a pan, cover with water and bring them to a boiling point. Then add salt and simmer gently for about 1/2 hour. Drain the meats and cut them in small pieces. Saute the meats with butter adding chopped onions and herbs. Stir continuously for a few minutes and then put them back into the broth. Simmer for about an hour until the meats are tender. Then add rice and boil for 15 minutes. In the meantime beat the eggs with lemon juice and a little cold water. Add a little of the broth at a time, put it all into the pan and stir well. You can reheat the *mayeritsa* but you should never allow it to boil because it will curdle.

GOING VEGETARIAN

The Greeks love *horta,* vegetables. Most Greek women would go to the fields and look for wild varieties. They are the great delicacies that would go practically with any dish. With fish and poultry and meat. Most popular are the *radikia* (dandelion), *vrouva* (mustard or charlock), *spanaki* (spinach), *kounoupidi* (cauliflower) and *antidia* (andives). But the varieties are practically non-ending and it takes an expert to recognize the best—the young and tender.

Greek women know when to go to the fields and gather each variety at the proper time, before they flower. Mostly in spring or early summer. Of course, in Greece, as in America, and practically any other place in the world, there is a great variety of vegetables and they all play an important role in the meal. Most of them are eaten as a salad, but they can be cooked in many different ways and served as a side dish. There is also a great variety of *ladera,* vegetables cooked with olive oil to serve as a main dish, during the many Lent periods when the Greeks go vegetarian.

Such vegetable dishes are usually prepared with *anginares* (artichokes), *bamies* (okra), *domates* (tomatoes), *melitzanes* (egg plant), *kolokithia* (squash), *spanaki* (spinach), *prassa* (leeks), *patates* (potatoes), *fasolakia* (string beans) and *koukia* (fava or broad beans) etc. etc.

Protein foods are always expensive and hard to get in Greece. As a result the Greeks developed unlimited ways of preparing vegetables. One could write a book on the preparation of squash alone. Greeks make even meatballs out of squash. They make soufles in a hundred different ways. They make little shoes and stuffed *kolokithia.*

And, of course, they fry and stew them. And they boil them to serve as a salad. In some areas they even make sweets out of squash. And Greeks have a say:

Ekato okades kolokithia ena drami dinami.

Which means 300 pounds of squash can give you a couple of grams of energy...

Boiled Squash / Kolokithakia Salata

Always use small and fresh squash in making a salad. No more than four inches long. Scrape them lightly and take out the flowers if you pick them from your garden. Drop them in salted water and cook for about ten minutes and drain them. Small ones do not need cutting into chunks. Dress with olive oil, lemon juice, salt and little black pepper.

Fried Squash / Kolokithia Tiganita

Larger squash can be used in frying. If very large slice them round, about a quarter of an inch. If medium size slice them very thin lengthwise. Have a batter ready, made of two tablespoons of flour, a well beaten egg, a pinch of baking soda, a couple of teaspoons of water, salt and a grind of black pepper. The squash should be fried very quickly in olive oil after you dip them in the batter and should be piled drained in a heated plate. If fresh, flowers also can be fried since they are delicious. *Kolokithia tiganita* is a favored dish and go well with *skordalia* sauce.

Squash Stew / Kolokithia Yahni

2 pounds squash
3 onions
1 pound
ripe tomatoes
1/2 cup olive oil
1 teaspoon each, sugar,
dill and mint
Salt and pepper

The squash should be medium size and the tomatoes ripe. If large *kolokithia* are used, cut them in half after trimming and scraping them. Fry lightly the onions in olive oil. Do not let them get brown, only soft. When you fry onions always keep in mind to slice them and not allow them to burn. Pass the tomatoes through a sieve and add them to the onions with a teaspoon of sugar. Cook for ten more minutes. Then, add 1/4 cup of water, season with salt and pepper and stir well. Now, put the squash in and add the herbs.
Continue to cook slowly until the squash gets tender. Use the same pan in frying the onions and cooking the squash. Let the stew cool a little, for about fifteen minutes, to settle, before serving. A most popular variation is the *briam*.

Baked Mixed Vegetables / Briam

2 pounds okra
1-1/2 pounds squash
2 large carrots
1 pound potatoes
2 onions
2 garlic cloves
1 can tomatoes
(28-ounce)
1/2 cup parsley
1 tablespoon oregano
1 cup olive oil
Salt and pepper

In an oiled casserole or baking platter place layers of potatoes, carrots, zucchini, onions and okra. Sprinkle each layer with salt, pepper, oregano, parsley, olive oil and garlic and pealed tomatoes. Top the casserole with tomato mixture and olive oil, cover with foil, and bake at 350° for 1 hour, or until the potatoes and carrots are tender. You may add eggplant, string beans or other fresh vegetables in season.

Stuffed Squash / Kolokithia Gemista

2 pounds squash
1 pound chopped meat,
beef or veal
1/2 pound chopped onions
1 can tomatoes
1/2 cup parsley and
mint leaves
1/2 cup rice
2 tablespoons butter
Salt and pepper

Use medium-sized squashes. Wash, scrape lightly, cut off ends and scoop out centers with a potato peeler, to form a tube. Do not scrape too close to the skin. Sprinkle with salt. Mix chopped meat with chopped onions and parsley. Add, rice, salt, pepper and about 4 tablespoons of the squash pulp, finely chopped. Stuff the squashes and place in a saucepan, pour tomato sauce over them, salt, pepper and butter. Simmer for about one hour and if necessary, add a little water for the sauce. Cover the saucepan and simmer until tender.

Stuffed Squash Egg Lemon / Kolokithia Gemista Avgolemono

A very popular way to make stuffed squash is the *avgolemono*. The dish is similar to the *dolmades*. First prepare and stuff the squashes as directed in the previous recipe. The two cups of water are substituted for tomatoes. Cover and cook until squashes are tender, then drain off al the liquid into a saucepan and bring it to a boil. Mix 3-4 tablespoons of flour with 1/2 cup cold milk. Add two eggs and the juice of one lemon. Stir and pour mixture into the boiling liquid, a little at a time, until it thickens like a cream. If it is too thin, add a teaspoon flour mixed with a little milk or water. The sauce should be thick enough to stay on the squash.

Squash Pie / Kolokithopitta

2 pounds squash
3 onions
1 pound tomatoes
1/2 cup olive oil

1/2 cup bread-crumbs
1/4 cup parsley
1/4 cup dill
Salt and pepper

Clean, scrape and slice the squash and the tomatoes rather thick. Brush your baking tin with olive oil and after you cover the bottom with a layer of squash, spread with thinly sliced onions adding tomato, bread-crumbs, herbs and seasoning. Repeat until all the ingredients are used. Make sure the distribution is even and tomatoes are on top. Pour olive oil and while baking in a moderate oven for about an hour or longer if necessary, until the vegetables are soft. If the pie has a tendency to get very dry add some tomato juice while cooking.

Squash Fritters / Kolokithokeftedes

2 pounds squash
3 potatoes
2 onions
1 egg
2 slices bread

1 cup grated cheese
1 dessertspoon parsley
1/2 teaspoon mint
Salt and
pepper

All the ingredients should be cut very finely. Potatoes should be boiled and the squash should be squeezed into pulp after boiling. The bread should be rather stale, soaked in a little water, after removing the crust and dried by squeezing it into your palm. After getting all the ingredients together add the grated cheese and the egg, beaten well. Use either *Kefalotiri* or parmesan cheese for better result. Tarn the ingredients until well mixed. The *keftedes* are made with a spoon, the desired size. Make them flat with your hands. Rub your hands with flour from time to time. *Kolokithokeftedes* should not be fried, like the meat *keftedes* until brown. Use hot olive oil and fry them only until golden. They should be served hot.

Squash Souffle / Kolokithia Souffle

1 pound squash
4 eggs
4 ounces grated cheese
4 ounces butter

3 tablespoons flour
1 cup milk
Nutmeg
Salt and pepper

Clean, scrape and slice the squash before boiling them in salted water until tender. Drain, well after mashing the squash into a puree. Let it dry for about an hour and then mix in the flour, egg yolks, butter, milk and grated cheese. You can use either *kefalotiri* or *kasseri*, or parmesan cheese, it does not make any difference. Mix well and season with a grate of nutmeg, salt and pepper. The egg whites should be beaten separately and folded into the mixture. Sprinkle the mixture with some grated cheese and cook in a very hot oven until the mixture is well risen and forms a crust, the souffle. Serve right from the oven.

Squash Slippers / Kolokithia Papoutsakia

2 pounds squash	6 ounces grated cheese
3 onions	1 cup white sauce
3 ounces bread-crumbs	1 tablespoon parsley
2 ounces butter	salt and
3 eggs	pepper

First chop the onions and cook them until soft in very little water. Add the bread crumbs, two eggs well-beaten, butter, chopped parsley and the cheese, *kefalotiri* or parmesan. Mix well and season. Cook the squash in boiling salted water for ten minutes, then drain, cool them and split them lengthwise. Use a small spoon or some other tool to remove a little of the pulp from the center of each half and fill the vacuum with some of the mixture evenly. Place the squash in a greased tin and cover with white sauce into which you have beaten the third egg. Sprinkle the tops with some grated cheese and bake in very hot oven until golden and fluffy, like the souffle.

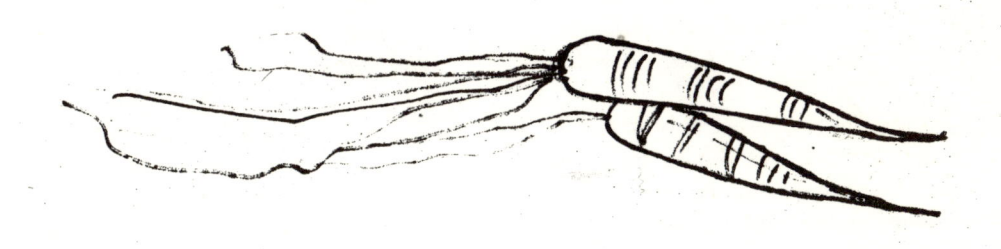

Fried Eggplant / Melitzanes Tiganites

2 pounds eggplant	salt and
1 egg	pepper

Cut the eggplant round if large, or slice it thinly lengthwise if medium, or small size. Let it drain in the sun sprinkled with salt. If there is no sun available, keep them in a warm spot. Heat or sun takes out the bitter liquid from the eggplant. Prepare a batter with flour and water and season it heavily. Add to the batter a well beaten egg and mix. Dry the eggplants, a slice at a time with a clean cloth, dip it in the batter and fry in very hot olive oil until they get golden and crisp. Like squash, *melitzanes tiganites* like a *skordalia* sauce the best.

Eggplant Stew / Melitzanes Stifatho

2 pounds eggplant
1 pound onions
1 pound tomatoes
1/2 cup olive oil
4 cloves garlic

2 tablespoons red wine
1 tablespoon sugar
1 bay leaf
Basil, salt
and pepper

Prepare the eggplant as in the previous recipe. Place them in a large pan and add the tomatoes, sliced. Use ripe tomatoes or in a can. Clean the onions and garlic, but do not slice them. Put them with the eggplants and add the sugar, olive oil, wine and herbs. Season and simmer slowly for about an hour. You may add some more water as you cook, but be careful not to make it too watery. Let it cool for a while before serving.

Artichokes In Oil / Anginares A La Polita

12 artichokes
3 carrots
12 small onions
1 pound small potatoes
1 cup olive oil

4 spring onions
4 lemons
1 tablespoon flour
dill, salt
and pepper

The artichokes, preferably small in size, should be thoroughly prepared. All tough outer leaves should be removed, the tops of the inner leaves sliced off and the stems trimmed down to about an inch, unless the artichokes are in season—young and tender, and underdeveloped—when even the hairy choke need not be removed. Have water ready in a bowl and add two tablespoons of flour, salt and the juice of a lemon. As you clean the artichokes rub them with half a lemon and throw them into the bowl, one by one, to prevent discolouring. *This is a standard manner of preparation for any kind of dish when artichokes are used.* Next put the onions into a large saucepan with a cup or more of water and bring to boil. Add the olive oil and seasoning (salt and pepper). Next put in the potatoes, carrots and artichokes, one at a time with their heads down. Add water to just cover. Place a piece of greaseproof paper to fit the saucepan, with a hole in the middle to let the the steam escape and place it over the artichokes. This, to obtain a good color. Cook for about ten minutes, sprinkle in a tablespoon of dill and continue to cook until the artichokes are tender. It takes about an hour. Remove the artichokes with care, arrange them on a serving dish and garnish with the onions, potatoes and carrots. To thicken the sauce, mix a teaspoon of flour with a little water and add it to the pan. Shake the pan gently, cook five minutes more, pour the sauce over the artichokes, and leave to cool.

Eggplant Slippers / Melitzanes Papoutsakia

2 pounds eggplant
4 onions
6 ounces cheese
1 egg
1 cup white sauce
2 tablespoons butter
olive oil
salt and pepper

First cut the eggplant in half lengthwise, sprinkle with salt and let them dry for about one hour. Next, fry them lightly in hot olive oil and arrange them cut-side up in a baking dish. Press the pulp down with a spoon to make a hollow in each half, season with salt and pepper and work with the filling. To prepare the filling chop the onions and cook until soft, in very little water. When half cooked add the butter and two tablespoons grated *kefalotiri* or parmesan cheese. Fill the hollowed eggplants with the mixture. Beat the egg into the white sauce and cover the eggplants. Sprinkle the rest of the grated cheese on top and brown in the oven. Finely minced meat may be added to the filling to make it a main dish. *Melitzanes papoutsakia* should be served hot.

Eggplant In Oil / Imam-Baildi

5 small eggplant
1 pound onions
1 cup oil
1 teaspoon sugar
4 tomatoes
2 or 3 cloves garlic
1 tablespoon parsley
salt and pepper

Wash and remove leaves and cut the stems of the eggplants. Make three or four lengthwise incisions in each eggplant, without separating the pieces. Sprinkle in between incisions with salt and let them settle to have the bitterness run out. Fry in oil until they start to wilt and then place in a baking dish, side by side, with some sliced onions in between the eggplants. Brown the rest of the onions lightly in the same oil. Add a little chopped parsley, salt, pepper, sugar, chopped garlic, and mix. Let cool a little and then stuff the incisions with this filling. Slice and place the tomatoes on top with the remaining of the parsley. Sprinkle with a little more salt, some dry bread crumbs and some oil from the pan. Bake in a moderate oven for about one hour. Do not serve very hot. Let them cool. The more the better.

Eggplant Pie / Moussaka

3-4 lb. eggplant
2 lb. minced meat
2 ripe tomatoes
2 lb. grated cheese (parmesan)
2 tablespoons grated onions
2 tablespoons chopped parsley
1 wineglass red wine

1/4 teaspoon cinnamon
1/4 teaspoon nutmeg
2 ounces butter
3 eggs
1-1/2 cup white sauce (bechamel)
salt and pepper
olive oil in frying

The magic ingredient of a true *moussaka* is the eggplant. You have to be very careful in their preparation. Slice them and sprinkle them with salt liberally. Let them drain for about 30 minutes in a colander. They lose bitterness. Rinse them good and pat dry them in a kitchen cloth. Fry a few at a time in hot olive oil until they brown on both sides. Drain them well and keep them warm as you proceed in another pan.

Melt the butter and work with the meat, adding gradually onions and sliced tomatoes, until the meat is *saute*. Parsley, spices, wine are added as you cook. Moisten with a little water, if necessary. After cooking for 20 minutes, you remove from the fire and stir in two tablespoons of the white sauce, prepared as indicated in the sauces recipe chapter.

Butter a baking-dish and fill with layers of eggplants and meat by alternating and springling each layer with grated cheese. You start and end with a layer of eggplant. Add three well beaten eggs to the sauce and pour over the dish. Sprinkle with the remaining grated cheese and some nutmeg and bake in a hot oven for about 45 minutes—until the top becomes golden brown.

There are many varieties of *moussaka*. Eggplant are substituted with potatoes, squash or artichokes. But, an authentic Greek *moussaka* is always made with eggplant.

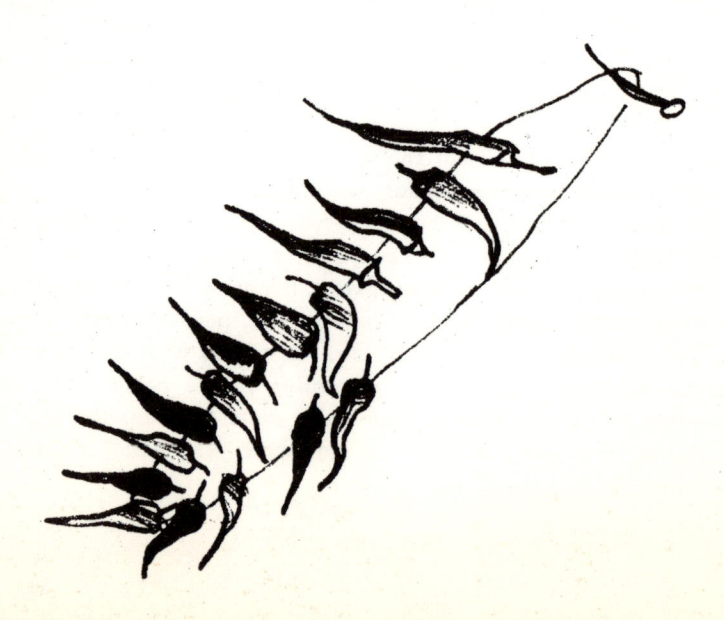

Fried Artichokes / Anginares Tiganites

8 artichokes
2 eggs
4 ounces bread-cumbs
1 lemon
olive oil
salt and pepper

Prepare the artichokes, small or no more than medium size, as in the previously explained manner. Cut them in half, lengthwise. Always rub them with lemon and leave them in the water for at least over an hour. In many areas tiny insects like to hide between the leaves and stubbornly stick, inspite a thorough washing. By soaking them into the water, you make sure all impurities are removed. Change the water and boil for half an hour. Beat the eggs with a teaspoon of lukewarm water until they become light. Have the bread-crumbs ready in a plate. After draining each artichoke dip it into the egg-mixture, then the bread-crumbs, again in the egg-mixture and fry in very hot and deep olive oil until they become golden brown. If you like, you may mix some grated cheese with the bread-crumbs.

Artichokes With Fava Beans / Anginares Me Koukia

12 artichokes
1-1/2 pounds fava beans
1 bunch of spring onions
1 cup olive oil
1 tablespoon lemon juice
3 tablespoons dill
1 teaspoon mint
salt and pepper

Prepare the artichokes in the previously prescribed manner. Put the beans, chopped onions and herbs into a wide, shallow pan with the olive oil and *saute* them gently for about ten minutes. Arrange the artichokes with the heads down, on the contents of the pan, season to taste, add the lemon juice and barely cover with water. Cut a round of greaseproof paper to fit the pan and press it gently down on the artichokes with a plate. Simmer very slowly for about one hour and leave to stand for at least half an hour before serving. If the beans are very young and fresh from the garden they need not be shelled. Trim and wash them and put into the pan whole. This dish is equally good, if garden peas are used instead of broad beans in which case add one tablespoon of sugar and, if liked, a chopped ripe tomato. Try to use young and fresh artichokes all the time. The smaller the tastier.

Stuffed Artichokes / Anginares Gemistes

10 artichokes
1 onion
2 cloves garlic
1 pound fresh or frozen fava beans
1 lemon
1/4 cup olive oil
3 sticks celery
parsley, dill, mint
salt and pepper

Prepare the artichokes as prescribed previously. Fry lightly in a teaspoon of olive oil the onions, finely chopped with the garlic, crushed. Chop finely a bunch of parsley, a handful of dill, a teaspoon of mint and the celery and mix them in a bowl with the fried onion and garlic, adding salt and pepper and half the remaining oil. Insert the mixture into the leaves of the artichokes. Put the artichokes into a saucepan, add water almost to cover, and the remaining oil, and cook slowly for half an hour. Add the beans and continue to cook for another half an hour or until they are tender. If using frozen beans cook them only for the length of time indicated on the packet. *Anginares gemistes* can be served either hot or cold. They are equally delicious.

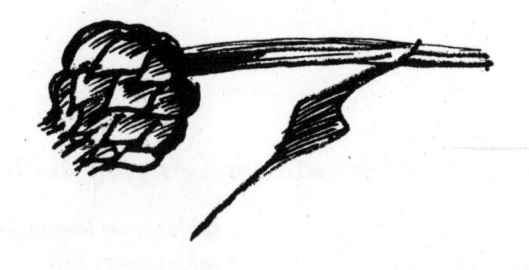

Artichokes Au Gratin / Anginares Au Gratin

10 artichokes
1 lemon
1/2 cup butter
2 cups white sauce
2 cups grated cheese
4 tablespoons bread-crumbs
salt and pepper

Clean the artichokes as previously indicated and put them into boiling salted water. Cover and cook over high heat until they are tender. Cut them into cubes, pour half the melted butter over them, and season. Prepare the white sauce. Butter a small pan and spread a thin layer of the sauce in it. Sprinkle generously with the cheese, spread the artichokes evenly on top and sprinkle additional cheese over them. Pour the remaining sauce over, then top with the rest of the cheese and the bread-crumbs. Drizzle the remaining butter over the top and bake in a preheated 350° oven for about 20 minutes or until golden brown.

Artichokes Salad / Anginares Salata

10 artichokes	1 lemon
6 small onions	1/4 cup olive oil
1 clove garlic	salt and
1/2 cup white wine	pepper

Prepare the artichokes as previously and let them stand for ten minutes in a bowl of boiling water. Put in a pan the onions, garlic, wine, lemon juice, olive oil, salt, pepper and then the artichokes, add boiling water to cover and cook for half an hour or until you can pull off the leaves easily. Take out the artichokes, turn them upside down to drain, then arrange on a dish. Reduce the liquid in which they have been cooked to about half or just a little less, add, if required, a little more salt and pepper and pour this, while still hot, over the artichokes. Leave until cold and add olive oil and lemon sauce.

Variations

Artichokes as practically all vegetables have many variations, like pickled etc. Most of these variations can be bought ready-made in cans at the food supermarket. Greek housewives use them extensively. Why shouldn't you?

Stuffed Tomatoes / Domates Gemistes

6 tomatoes medium-size	1 tablespoon
1 cup rice	pine cone nuts
1 cup olive oil	2 tablespoons parsley
3 onions	2 tablespoons mint
1 tablespoon raisins	salt and pepper

Wash the tomatoes and cut a thin slice from the bottom and keep to use later as caps after stuffing the tomatoes. Scoop out seeds and some of the pulp of the tomatoes and sprinkle the inside with a little salt and sugar. Set aside overturned so that they drain. Fry the onions finely chopped in olive oil until golden brown. Cut the pulp of tomatoes and mix with the onions. Cook a few minutes and add the rice and other ingredients. Mix well and stuff the tomatoes, using a teaspoon. Cover with caps, arrange in rows in a baking dish, pour on a little more olive oil, and sprinkle with dry bread crumbs. Bake in moderate oven. *Domates Gemistes* taste better when served cold.

Greek housewives stuff their tomatoes in an infinite way. They add *kima* to the stuffing or they substitute *kima* with shrimps, eggplant, or they add raisins to the rice. Unless your husband and guests appreciate your expertise in fancy cooking we suggest that you concentrate in the basic ways of preparing Greek dishes and reserve your urge for originality for later on. One should always know the rules before thinking about amendments.

Tomato Omelet / Omeleta Me Domates

1 1/2 pounds ripe tomatoes
salt and pepper
4 tablespoons butter
6 eggs

This is a delicious dish you can make in a jiffy.
Wash and peel the tomatoes, scoop out the seeds, cut into small pieces, place in a frying pan with a little salt and pepper and cook until reduced to a pulp. Add the butter, beat the eggs with salt and pepper, and pour into the pan. Allow to cook slowly and stir gently. Serve immediately. Excellent with fried potatoes and especially if you add a few chunks of *feta* cheese while the butter is browning and before you pour the beaten eggs.

Stuffed Peppers / Piperies Gemistes

Stuffed peppers as a rule are simply a companion of stuffed tomatoes and therefore the same stuffing is used. To prepare the peppers cut the top about an inch and use it as a cap. Remove the seeds and cores from the inside and boil them until they soften a little, before stuffing. Use green peppers.

String Beans In Oil / Fassolakia Yahni

2 pounds string beans
1 pound tomatoes
1 onion
1 cup olive oil
Parsley, sugar,
salt and pepper

First peel and chop the tomatoes and onion. Trim the beans, snap them into halves if they are very long but do not slice them thinly. Heat the olive oil, lightly fry the onion add the beans and simmer until they begin to soften. Then add the tomatoes, salt, pepper and parsley, a little sugar and just enough water to cover. Continue to cook slowly until the beans are tender, about 40 minutes.
String beans as most of the vegetables are a usual companion of fish, meat and poultry. In many cases Greek housewives cook them in the same pan with the meat for added taste. Greek-American housewives and restaurants prefer to cook the vegetable separately and serve them as a side dish. When the recipe calls for mixing with meat, like in *fricasse*, you will be guided accordingly.

Beans Stew / Fassolia Yahni

1 pound navy beans	2 celery sticks
1 cup olive oil	1/2 cup parsley
1/2 cup tomato paste	1 teaspoon sugar
3 onions	salt and
2 carrots	pepper

The beans should be soaked overnight. Boil in four cups of fresh water until tender.
Fry chopped onions in oil until golden brown. Add the tomato sauce, diced carrots, minced celery, parsley, salt, pepper and a teaspoon of sugar. Simmer until cooked. Drain the beans and add the sauce. Simmer for another 15 minutes. Add a little of bean water, enough to keep the dish not too dry. If desired, fry the onion in butter instead of in olive oil.

Giant Beans Oil-Tomato / Gigantes Plaki

1 1/2 pounds giant navy beans	2 garlic cloves
1 1/2 pounds onions	1 teaspoon sugar
1 1/2 pounds tomatoes	2 tablespoons mint
1 cup of olive oil	salt and pepper

This is a very common *meze* dish in Greek tavernas. The giant navy beans should be soaked overnight. In the morning cook them rapidly in water for 5 minutes, drain, return them to the stove with fresh salted water and leave to cook until they are tender. Again thoroughly drain them, keep the water, and in this cook the finely chopped onions for 5 minutes. Now drain off the water from the onions and add a quarter of the olive oil and cook the onions in this until they begin to brown. Add the beans, peeled and finely chopped, tomatoes, chopped garlic, remaining oil, salt, pepper, sugar and mint, also finely chopped. Continue cooking very slowly for another half hour.
Instead of fresh tomatoes you can use thick tomato juice. The quantity of mint can be reduced to taste, or, if preferred, use parsley.

Okra/Bamies

1 1/2 pound okra
1 tablespoon parsley
1 onion
1 garlic clove
1 can whole tomatoes
(8-ounce)

1 cup olive oil
2 tablespoons white wine
or vinegar
salt and pepper

Trim the okra cones after washing. Place them in a bowl, sprinkle them with vinegar, and let them stand for two hours. Rinse them thoroughly in cold water.

Saute minced onions and garlic and chopped parsley in olive oil. Add tomatoes, wine and cook a few minutes more. Then add okra and spoon sauce over them. Season with salt and pepper; cover and simmer until tender. Okra goes well with lamb dishes, or broiled chicken.

Potatoes Oil-Tomato/Patates Yahni

3 pounds potatoes
1 pound onions
1 pound tomatoes

1/2 cup
olive oil
salt and pepper

This is a very common way to prepare potatoes as a companion to meat dishes. After washing and peeling the potatoes cut them into fairly uniform size. Heat the oil and fry the onions until they are a golden brown. The onions should be chopped, as usual. Add the tomatoes, also peeled and chopped. Simmer until soft, then add the potatoes, salt and pepper and enough hot water to cover. Cook until the potatoes are soft and the sauce thick. You can substitute olive oil with cooking fat or butter.

Potato Fritters / *Patatokeftedes*

6 potatoes
2 eggs
3 ounces
grated cheese

3 ounces flour
1 tablespoon butter
olive oil
salt and pepper

First peel, boil and mash the potatoes. Beat the eggs well and mix with the grated cheese. Add seasoning. Have the flour ready on a pad. Make a mixture of all ingredients and form round flat cakes, not too thick. Pat them firmly on the flour before frying in very hot oil. Use *kefalotiri* or parmesan cheese. Serve hot as they come out of the frying pan.

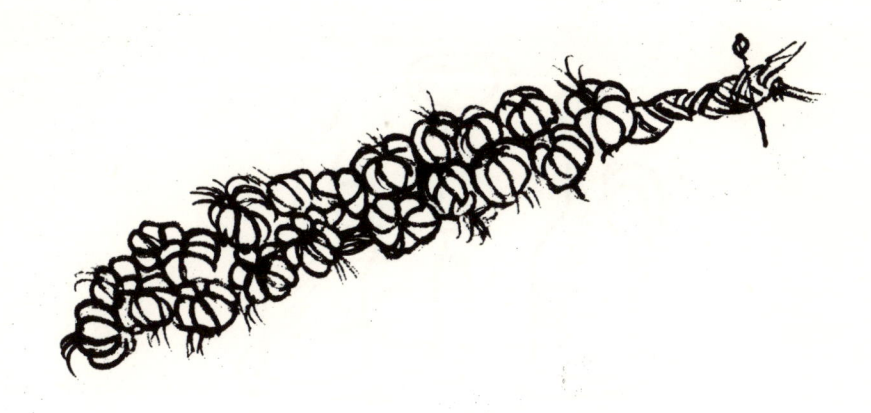

Spinach With Rice / *Spanakorizo*

3 pounds spinach
3 onions
6 ounces rice

1/2 cup olive oil
Dill, salt
and pepper

First saute lightly the onions, chopped in olive oil. Use a large saucepan and do not let the onions get colored. When half cooked, add the spinach, washed thoroughly and cleaned from all foreign substances. Simmer gently for about five minutes with the saucepan covered and then add a tablespoon of chopped dill, seasoning and water to cover. When you bring it to boil add the rice and stir well, once, with a wooden spoon. Cook on a brisk fire until the water is reduced and the rice swells. Take it off from the fire as soon as the water has been absorbed. You can leave it on a very low fire until the rice is cooked and the water completely absorbed. Let it settle for 10-15 minutes before serving, but be careful to not let the steam completely out. Cover with a clean cloth when you take the lid.

Cauliflower Oil Tomato / Kounoupidi Yahni

*2 medium size
cauliflowers
2 large onions
1 can tomato juice
and pepper
2 garlic cloves
2 ounces olive oil
Parsley, salt*

Wash thoroughly the cauliflower, remove the coarse stalks and separate the flowerets. Heat the oil and fry the onions, finely chopped and the pounded garlic until a golden brown. Add the tomato juice, salt, pepper and a handful of finely chopped parsley and bring this to boil. Add the cauliflower and cook until tender. Serve the sauce separately. It can be thickened with flour if necessary.

Cauliflower Au Gratin / Kounoupidi Au Gratin

*1 medium-size cauliflower
2 cups white sauce
1 egg
2 tablespoons butter
1/2 cup grated cheese
1/2 lemon
1/4 teaspoon nutmeg
salt and pepper*

Wash and remove stem from cauliflower and boil in salted water. Add lemon juice to keep it white. Cook until just tender. Do not overcook. It will make it mushy. Separate into flowerets and place them in a buttered dish. Then add to the white sauce one beaten egg, nutmeg, salt and pepper. Mix well, pour over the cauliflower, sprinkle with grated cheese and melted butter and bake in a hot oven (400°F) for about 20-25 minutes until lightly browned.

Stuffed Cabbage / Dolmades Me Lahano

1 large cabbage
3 tomatoes
6 ounces rice
2 onions
2 garlic cloves
1 tablespoon pine-nuts
1 tablespoon raisins
3 tablespoons olive oil
cinnamon and flour
salt and pepper

First heat the oil and cook the rice for 3 minutes. Add the onions, finely chopped, the garlic crushed, the raisins and pine-nuts. Stir and let the ingredients cook slowly until golden brown. Add the tomatoes, cinnamon, salt and pepper. Continue simmering very slowly. In the meantime prepare the cabbage leaves. Choose fairly large and fresh ones. Blanch them in boiling water to make them pliable. Spread them on a table and trim away the thick centre vein. This makes the leaves easier to roll. Put a small portion of the stuffing on to each leaf, roll it up carefully, tucking in the edges as described for *Dolmades*. Keep the *dolmades* close together in a saucepan, cover with salted water or tomato juice, sprinkle with lemon juice and place an upturned plate over them to keep them steady. If the *dolmades* have plenty of space they will swim around and possibly break. Cover with the saucepan lid and cook very slowly for 3/4 of an hour. Take the *dolmades* from the pan when cooked, keep them hot while you thicken the sauce—this can be done with cream or with a flour and water paste. The *dolmades* and their sauce should be served separately.

Endives Egg-Lemon / Antidia Avgolemono

4 bunches endives
2 eggs
2 lemons
1 cup broth
1/4 cup butter
salt and pepper

Use very cold water to soak the endives, cut in half, for about fifteen minutes. This makes them crisp and takes out some of their bitterness. Dry them with a white cloth. Melt the butter in a pan and put the endives in.
Add salt and pepper and a tablespoon lemon juice. Brown for a couple of minutes the endives on each side and add the broth little by little. Simmer uncovered, for half an hour or until tender. Make the *avgolemono* sauce and pour over the endives.

Boiled Greens / Horta Vrasta

<table>
<tr><td>Mixed greens</td><td>Lemon juice</td></tr>
<tr><td>Olive oil</td><td>Salt</td></tr>
</table>

Always use fresh greens, dandelion, mustard, rapini, escarole, endive, spinach. Wash greens several times, drain them, place them in salted boiling water, and boil until tender. Most greens require about 20 minutes cooking, the dandelions slightly longer, and the mustard greens even longer; so start these earlier. Remove from water, but do not drain. Place in a bowl, and serve with oil and lemon juice.

Boiled vegetables, of practically every kind, are served as a side dish or with sauce. For instance, boiled *pantzaria* (beets) are very popular with *scordalia* sauce. *Piperies* are also popular fried as a *meze*.

If you use your vegetables intelligently you can skip main dishes and a lot of weight along with cooking headaches.

GETTING FAT

Not all Greeks are vegetarians. As a matter of fact Greeks have many different mannerisms at the same time in their eating habits. They love vegetables and prepare them in an unending variety of ways, as we have indicated in our previous chapter. But they also love their fish, meat and poultry, their cheese and spices, their salads and soups. And they are *"saltsades"*— sauce lovers.

Greeks call Italians *"makaronades"*, because Italians are notorious for their love for macaroni. Yet, no people love more than the Greeks a *makaronada*, toppled with rich meat sauce or hot butter and lots and lots of grated *kefalotiri* or parmesan.

There is nothing wrong with a soup-plate filled with a mountain of rich *makaronada*, just taken out of the fire and generously sprinkled with hot butter and grated cheese. Only, keep in mind a Greek *makaronada* is not quite the best diet to lose weight. It tops the scale to the plus.

If you are on a diet to lose weight a good way to do it is to go straight to the next chapter and forget about dishes in this one altogether.

Macaroni and rice dishes, as Greeks prepare them, help you get fat and fill an already extended tummy...

THE SPAGHETTI

Greeks prepare their spaghetti or noodles dishes pretty much the same way as the Italians. Probably the only difference is their *pasticcio*, which plays an important role in their *mezes* and menus—like the *ravioli* in the Italian menus.

Basically Greeks eat their spaghetti either "white" with plenty of very hot butter and grated *kefalotiri* on top, or with *kima,* meat sauce:

Spaghetti / Makaronada

2 1/2 pounds spaghetti	1 tablespoon tomato paste
1 pound minced meat	3 garlic cloves
3 onions	1/2 cup olive oil
1 glass white wine	1 bay leaf
6 ounces grated cheese	Cinnamon and sugar
1 1/2 pounds tomatoes	Salt and pepper

First make the sauce. Chop the onions finely and cook them gently in a little water and olive oil. Add the minced meat and stir with a wooden spoon to prevent burning. Add the tomatoes, ripe and sieved, tomato paste, sliced garlic, bay leaf, cinnamon and sugar. Season with salt and pepper and stew gently for an hour. The sauce should be thick by then. Keep the wine to add last to the sauce, ten minutes before serving.

Boil the spaghetti in boiling salted water and drain. Return to the pan and toss in it butter. Pile on a serving dish and sprinkle with grated cheese. Serve the sauce separately with a dish of grated cheese.

To make "white" spaghetti use half a pound of butter for each pound of spaghetti or noodle. Do not use olive oil in spaghetti. Use either *kefalotiri* or parmesan type in all dishes calling for grated cheese.

Spaghetti Chopped Meat / Pasticcio

1 1/2 pound spaghetti	2 tablespoons tomato paste
1 pound chopped meat	
1 cup butter	1 glass white wine
1 can tomatoes	1 cup chopped onions
1 cup grated cheese	1 cup white sauce
1 cup bread crumbs	Nutmeg, salt and pepper

First boil the spaghetti. Be careful not to overcook. Drain and return to the saucepan. Add half of the butter or fat.

Prepare the *kima* sauce or filling with the above ingredients as directed in recipe for *kima* sauce.

Add 3 unbeaten egg whites and half of the cheese to macaroni, and mix well. Butter a baking dish or pan and sprinkle bottom with the dried bread crumbs. Add macaroni. Spread the *kima* sauce, to which 1/2 cup dried bread crumbs have been added.

Cover with a white sauce Bechamel to which 3 unbeaten egg yolks, part of the cheese and nutmeg have been added. Sprinkle with the rest of the grated cheese, some more bread crumbs to form a crust and pour over the rest of the warm butter.

Bake in a hot oven for 40-45 minutes until golden brown.

Cool slightly, cut into square pieces and serve.

Spaghetti Au Gratin / Makaronia Au Gratin

1 pound spaghetti	4 tablespoons flour
5 ounces butter	1/4 pound grated cheese
2 eggs	Nutmeg
2 cups milk	Salt and pepper

Boil the spaghetti in salted water, drain and reserve two cups of drained water. Return to saucepan and pour melted butter over it. Make a thick white sauce by bringing the milk to a boil, using the water reserved from the spaghetti and adding the flour. Mix with a wire beater, to prevent lumps. Add salt, nutmeg, eggs and a little cheese.

In a well-buttered casserole spread a thin layer of the sauce and add the spaghetti and some cheese. Add the remaining sauce, sprinkle with more cheese and top with melted butter. Bake for about half an hour.

Spaghetti Timbale / Makaronia Me Bacon

2 pounds thin spaghetti	4 tablespoons butter
2 cups grated cheese	3 eggs
8 slices bacon, or	1/2 cup bread-crumbs
4 sausages	Salt, pepper and nutmeg

First, cook spaghetti in boiling salted water, drain and return to saucepan. Pour melted butter over it and mix with the spaghetti either the grated cheese or feta crumbled if desired. Cut the bacon sausages into small pieces and add to the spaghetti. Add salt, pepper and nutmeg. Beat the eggs and add them too. Mix well, grease a deep circular cake pan and dust it with pounded bread crumbs. Fill with the spaghetti mixture and bake in a moderate oven for half an hour. Cool for 15 minutes and overturn into a serving platter.

Orzo / Kritharaki

1/2 pound kritharaki	2 ounces tomato paste
5 ounces butter	3 onions
5 ounces grated cheese	1 bay leaf
	Salt and pepper

Kritharaki is not barley. It is a pasta made like makaroni, noodles or *hilopites* and *trahana*. In Greek countryside *kritharaki* is always home-made. However Italian and Greek groceries always have excellent qualities of *pasta*.

Fry the onions in butter until golden brown. Add water, diluted tomato paste or fresh tomatoes, salt, pepper and a bay leaf. Simmer for fifteen minutes and add the *kritharaki*. Stir with a wooden spoon a few times until it starts to boil and lower the flame. Simmer until all the liquid is absorbed and *kritharaki* is cooked. Serve on a platter and sprinkle with grated *kefalotiri* or parmesan.

Orzo With Meat / Giuvetsi

2 pounds lamb	3 tablespoon tomato paste
1 pound orzo	3 tablespoons onion
1 cup butter	Salt and pepper

Although this recipe belongs to the meat categories, I include it here to give you an idea of the role spaghetti, noodles or orzo play in *giuvetsi*. The preparation of the pasta is the same with any kind you choose.

First clean the lamb and cut it in pieces. Brown the meat in butter along with the minced onion. Place in enough water to cover the meat, add the tomato diluted in a glass of water. Season and cook for half an hour. Add orzo and stir two or three times until it starts to boil slowly. Cover and cook until the pasta is ready and the meat is tender. Add a little water if the liquid is absorbed before the pasta cooked. Grated cheese may be sprinkled on top, if you like it.

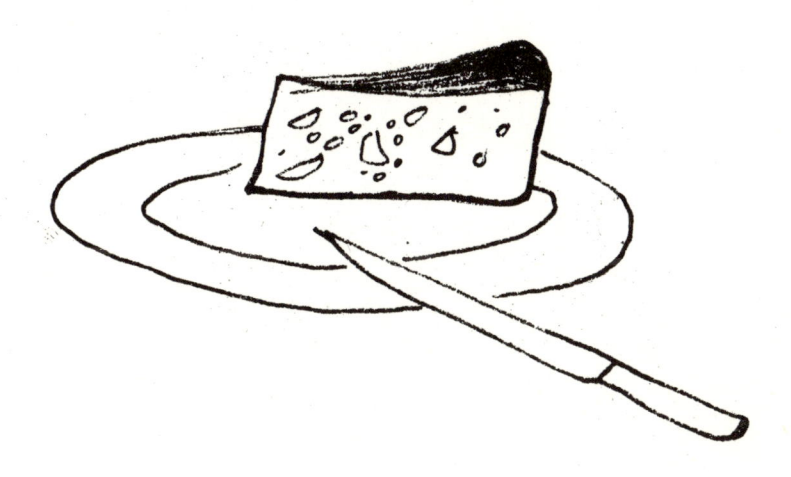

THE "PILAFAS"

A fat man who cannot move his body or brain swiftly around is called *"pilafas"* (rice eater) by the Greeks. Turks are notorious *"pilafas"* in the sense that they love rice very much. Most of the variations in cooking rice are based on a standard *pilafi* recipe. If you can prepare a good standard *pilafi* you can prepare every *pilafi* variation.

Rice Pilaf / Pilafi

2 cups rice	4 tablespoons butter
4 cups stock	Salt

Over a brisk fire melt 1 1/2 tablespoon of butter in a saucepan and then add the water hot and salted. When the water reaches the boiling point throw in the rice and stir well. Stir only once to prevent the rice from shackling. Boil until the rice swells and the water evaporates. As the water is absorbed by the rice or evaporates, use a clean cloth to cover the saucepan, turn the fire to very low and let simmer for half an hour. Before serving melt the remaining butter, pour over the rice and place in form.

In making *pilafi*, the Greeks usually use a stock that best complements the dish with which they are serving it. For example, they use a chicken stock for fowl entrees, a clam broth for fish dishes, and a beef stock for beef and heavy meats. Some of the pan juices in which the main meat dish was cooked may also be substituted for part of the liquid. The only important rule is that the proportions of liquid to rice, 2 to 1, always remain the same.

Shrimps With Rice / Pilafi Me Garides

3 dozens shrimps	1/2 wineglass cream
2 cups rice	2 garlic cloves
1 onion	1 teaspoon sugar
2 ounces butter	Cinnamon, rosemary
1 cup tomato pulp	or basil
1/2 wineglass vermouth	Salt and pepper

The shrimps should be boiled as indicated in the pertinent recipe. Take out the shrimp heads. Chop the onion and garlic very finely and *saute* gently in butter until quite soft. Add the tomato pulp, sugar, a pinch of cinnamon, a spring of rosemary or basil and season with salt and pepper. Simmer slowly for half an hour, remove from the fire and pass through a fine sieve. Return to the pan and put in the shrimps with the vermouth and cream and reheat. Have ready the *pilafi*. Press the rice into a ring mould or some form before turning out on to the serving dish. Fill the center with the shrimps. Serve hot.

Rice With Octopus / Htapodhi Pilafi

1 small octopus
6 ounces rice
1 onion
1/4 cup olive oil

2 tomatoes
1 dessertspoon tomato paste
Salt and pepper

First wash the octopus well, remove the ink sac and keep it. Cut into small pieces and put into a pan without water. Leave over a small flame to draw the liquid from the octopus. When the liquid has been absorbed add a finely chopped onion and olive oil and cook gently for ten or fifteen minutes. Next add the chopped and skinned tomatoes or the tomato paste diluted with water and the ink from the octopus. Add enough water to cover and cook until the octopus is quite tender. Throw in the rice and cook rapidly until all the liquid in the pan has been absorbed. Place a dry clean cloth over the pan when removing the cover and let it settle for about ten minutes before serving.

Varieties

Pilafi goes well with quite a number of main dishes. It goes well with chicken livers and calf's liver. It makes a very tasty dish with ham or spinach (see *spanakorizo*) or any kind of vegetable. It is delicious with all sorts of poultry. It is a very tasty companion to shrimps, lobster or octopus and squids, but it is rarely served with other kinds of fish. Always keep in mind there are two standard ways to prepare rice—the same as in spaghetti: "White," with hot butter and plenty of grated *kefalotiri* or parmesan and "red," with tomato or meat sauce. The rest are simply additions to turn a *pilafi* from a side dish to a main course.

PART III

"ELA STO PSITO"

Bid them come now, and not delay
Nor vex the cook who's ready for them.
For all the fish is long since boiled,
And all the roast meats long since cold.

Athenaeus

PART III

PLASTICITY

"*Ela sto psito*" in Greek means "get to the point." *Psito,* baked lamb or beef, is the main Greek dish and therefore getting to the *psito* is simply getting to the point. The expression is used widely to help someone skip the trivia and "come to the meat." The "point" here was made eloquently by Aristophanes :

> *No more anchovy for me... Rather, bring me a piece of liver or a glandule from a young boar, or failing that, a rib or a tongue or a spleen; or fetch me the paunch of a suckling-pig killed in the autumn, with some hot rolls."*

Those who have read Homer's *Odyssey* and visit the Greek countryside today can still recognize the hills and valleys, the mud houses with fences of piled stones, the olive trees and the vineyards, the orange, lemon, apple and chesnut trees irrigated by rivets coming down from the mountainous fountains and springs, through woods of pine, cypress and cedar, among clusters of multicolored flowers, beds of violets and parsley, exactly as Homer so extensively describes them. Of course, lions have being long extinct and you will rarely see an owl, a hawk or a bat, or even a wolf or those brightly colored birds of the Homeric times. Yet, horses and mules and donkeys still draw carts along shady lanes. And everyday activity in the countryside is now as then concentrated around food, one way or another. Even evening activities in the islands and ports are connected with food as the fishermen get to the seas for the night's toil.

Fish, meat and poultry make the "point" in Greek cookery and our adventure of necessity takes us through the familiar places Homer minutely described in his "Odysseus wanderings." Sex and food dominate his narrative and no writer of the antiquity illustrated more clearly the butchering of pig, to use one of the many detailed descriptions in the *Odyssey.* "First a hard blow on the head, then the knife at the throat and the immediate quartering. The fat trimmed, dipped in barley soup and thrown into the fire to feed the gods while the rest goes to the spit for a quick cooking and eating."

Ancient Greeks apparently had abundant food, beef, mutton, pork, cheese, milk and olives aplenty. Meat of all kinds was prepared on spits and heaped on great platters; fish broiled; wine flowing freely; and bread, and fruits and honey—the *ambrosia* and *nektar* of gods.

A knife was all ancient Greeks needed to eat. Cutting a piece of meat if they could not pick it up with their hands directly from the platter. They would rather sip their soups and liquids, and therefore no spoons were needed and there was hardly any need for a fork. Their fingers and their knife could do the job beautifully.

Getting familiar with the eating habits of ancient Greeks as described by Homer in *Odyssey* and Athenaeus in the *Deipnosophists*, one becomes fascinated when visiting Greece today and recognizing not only the places but the habits as well, preserved through the ages by customs and traditions transferred from generation to generation and kept a dear heritage.

As you travel through the Greek countryside you need no imagination to reconstitute life as it used to be. The landscape is there, the mountains, the rivers, the valleys, the rocks, rising, flowing. And scattered among them cattle—goats, burrows, pigs, cows, poultry, horses, dogs and more sheep than people. Lamb therefore is the main dish in the rural diet, but a Greek herder can go for days on bread and olives and a Greek fisherman on a bowl of *kakavia* provided there is *retsina* to help "wash the throat."

> *"By God, although a song's immortal, it's a beast*
> *and needs lean meat to strengthen, wine to spout and roar*
> *All are the belly's woof, my lads, and bread's the warp,*
> *the body is a whirring loom that never rests."*
>
> Kazantzakis : The Odyssey IXX, 1385

Roast Lamb / Arni Psito

3 pounds leg or shoulder
of lamb
1/2 cup olive oil
1 teaspoon oregano

2 tablespoons lemon juice
4 cloves garlic
Rosemary
salt and pepper

This is the standard Greek dish. After cleaning the meat make incisions to insert the garlic cloves and a little rosemary in it. Rub the meat with juice of half a lemon, olive oil and salt and pepper. Place the meat in a roasting-tin and pour over it the rest of the olive oil and the lemon juice. Sprinkle generously with oregano, salt and pepper and add a cup of water. You can add potatoes if you like. Select 6 large ones, peel them, cut them into four pieces each and surround the meat. Use a hot oven to cook and add more water if it is necessary, until the *arni* is tender. The potatoes must absorb all the water and be nicely browned.

A variation with chestnuts instead of potatoes makes a delicious dish too. In such case boil the chestnuts before peeling and omit garlic and oregano.

Lamb Pilaf / Arni Pilafi

2 pounds boneless lamb stew,
cut in 2-inch cubes
2 medium onions,
finely chopped
1/4 pound butter
1 can tomato (6-ounce)

1 tablespoon chopped parsley
1/4 teaspoon cinnamon
2 bay leaves
1/4 cup white wine
1 cup rice pilafi
salt and pepper

First brown the onions and parsley in butter; add the lamb and brown well over medium fire. Season with salt and pepper and add tomato paste, wine, cinnamon and bay leaves. Stir well. Add enough water or stock to cover the meat; cover pot with lid and simmer until the lamb is tender, about 1 hour, then remove the bay leaves. Make the *pilafi* using 1/2 cup of the sauce from the lamb cooking pot for 1/2 cup of the stock or water, and form into molds. Serve the lamb *saute* and the *pilafi* molds with tomato sauce from the lamb spooned over the *pilafi*.

Baked Lamb With Noodles / Giuvetsi Hilopites

3 pounds shoulder or
leg of lamb
2 pounds ripe tomatoes
4 tablespoons butter
1 tablespoon olive oil

1 pound noodles, macaroni
or hilopites
1 tablespoon lemon juice
1 teaspoon sugar
Salt and pepper

This traditional Greek dish owes its name to the fact that, even today, is cooked in a clay casserole called *giuvetsi*. You can cook the meat whole or cut to pieces and you can use any type of macaroni, noodles or square cut noodles, called *hilopites* in Greek.

First rub the meat well with a mixture of olive oil, lemon juice, salt and pepper. Place into a roasting-tin. Add two tablespoons of butter and cook for about an hour in moderate oven. Prepare a sauce with pulped tomatoes, 2 tablespoons of butter, sugar, and seasoning. Add about a pint of boiling water and when the sauce is bubbling throw in the macaroni and cook for about 10 minutes. Stir frequently and add more pulped tomatoes and water to prevent the macaroni from sticking together and become dry.

Do not overcook because the macaroni will absorb the liquid. Put the macaroni into the *giuvetsi* when it is partly cooked and continue to cook until a light crust is formed on top of the noodles or macaroni.

Lamb Fricasse / Arni Fricasse

3 pounds stewing lamb
4 heads lettuce or endive
2 ounces butter
1 large bunch of spring onions

2 tablespoons chopped dill
1 teaspoon chopped mint
Egg and lemon sauce
Salt and pepper

You can use a variety of vegetables instead of lettuce or endive to prepare this very delicious Greek dish. Artichokes or even fresh beans make good *fricasse*. First wash and cut the lamb into serving portions. Chop the onions including the green part and break the lettuce into pieces as if for salad. Melt the butter in a large saucepan and saute the lamb for 15 minutes. Add the onions, herbs and lettuce. Cook for 10 more minutes and add seasoning. Cover with water and simmer slowly for about 1 1/2 hour until the meat is tender. Add the egg and lemon sauce and serve hot.

Braised Lamb / Kokkinisto

3 pounds lamb	garlic
3 ounces butter	1/2 glass
1 large onion	white wine
A bayleaf	salt and pepper

Kokkinisto Arni is a classic dish that goes well with all vegetables. With tomatoes or squash, with fresh or dry beans, with egg-plant or okra, with celery or artichokes, with macaroni or rice, and even with chestnuts or olive oils.

The meat should be wiped with a damp cloth and then cut to serving portions. Put the meat in a saucepan with hot butter and let it brown. Add the onion chopped finely and continue frying until light golden. Then add gradually the wine and water enough to cover the bottom of the pan. Next add salt, pepper, garlic and the bay-leaf and cook over a medium fire until the meat is so tender it will break easily with a fork.

Most Greeks prefer to put the green vegetables, potatoes, rice or cauliflower in the *kokkinisto* for added flavour. In such a case put the vegetables or macaroni in with the meat 1/2 an hour before it is ready. You can also add a handful of chopped parsley.

Lamb Roast In Paper / Exohiko

2-3 pounds leg or shoulder of lamb	2 pounds k a s s e r i cheese
4 tablespoons olive oil	oregano
1 lemon juice	sliced garlic
	salt and pepper

You need 4-6 pieces of cooking paper large enough to hold portions of the lamb. Cut the portions after you clean the lamb and rub them generously with an olive oil and lemon juice sauce adding salt and pepper and oregano. Make incisions into the meat and insert slices of garlic. After lightly oiling the cooking paper place a portion of the lamb on each and top with a slice of *kasseri*. Wrap carefully the lamb portion and twist the side ends to make sure none of the juice escapes. Baste the package with olive oil, place in roasting pan and bake in a moderate fire for 3-4 hours. No water, no oil must be added. The pan should not be covered and the pieces should be close together and should not be turned over. Serve hot in the paper to retain the flavour and aroma.

Peasant Style Baked Lamb / Horiatiko

2 pounds breast or
shoulder of lamb
1 pound feta cheese

2 pounds tomatoes
2 tablespoon olive oil
salt and pepper

This is a variety of roast lamb. Many Greek tavernas serve it daily because it is one of the most popular—and easy—ways to prepare a tasty lamb dish. As always, you first wash and wipe the meat with a damp cloth. Cut it into large pieces and put them in a baking pan. Peel and slice the tomatoes, cut the cheese into small cubes and arrange them on top of the meat. Sprinkle with salt and pepper and olive oil, after you cover with the tomatoes. Bake in moderate fire until the meat is very tender. Do not turn the meat but baste from time to time. You can flavour with garlic if you like. Vegetables, rice or macaroni—or all of them—go well as a side dish with *horiatiko*.

Easter Lamb / Arni Sti Souvla

This is another Greek classic and a must for every home in the countryside on Easter Sunday. But you can do it on special occasions in your garden or backyard. Try to find a baby lamb if available. Larger ones are hard to cook. Make a small ditch on the ground, the length of the lamb. You need a spit with a handle to turn and two iron sticks with special holders that allow to lower the lamb as you proceed.

Have the butcher prepare the whole lamb by removing the intestines, entrails, and larynx, leaving only the kidneys, and cutting two holes in the back, level with the kidneys. Salt the lamb inside and out. Secure it on the spit, starting from the tail end and working toward the head; tie the back of the lamb to the spit to keep the meat taut. Sew up the cavity with a thick needle. Bring the rear and front legs up, and tie them to the spit. Rub the entire surface of the lamb with lemon juice. It is best to use a spit that can be adjusted in height. Start the lamb up high and gradually lower it toward the heat as the cooking progresses. During the cooking, baste the meat with oil or butter and, occasionally, with lemon juice. Keep the heat stronger toward the rear portion of the lamb, as this takes longer to cook. Toward the end of the cooking you may add some oregano to the basting fluids. The lamb is done when the meat separates easily from the bone.

Lamb-On-A-Spit / Gyros

This is a dish hard to make at home. But you can always call an expert cook to prepare it for you in your garden for a special occasion.
The meat—usually lamb—is cut from the rump into long strips, highly flavoured with garlic, herbs and spices and wound round a spit or long skewer. The spit is usually about three feet high and the width of the meat across the top ten inches and at the base three inches—the shape of an enormous spinning-top. The spit is fixed in a vertical position with a special charcoal fire divided in vertical sections with opening in front. A vertical electric heater can also be used but it can never bring the same results. The only electricity should be used is one to make the spit revolve in front of the charcoal fire while the lamb is cooking. You need a very sharp knife to carve the meat vertically in thin slices. You let the slices drop into a small tin pan with a handle. Carve only the cooked meat leaving the raw under layer exposed to the fire to continue cooking. The meat must be always nicely grilled. As you carve the *gyros* gets smaller and smaller until is nothing left but the spit.
Put each portion of *gyros* on a bed of finely sliced onion and chopped parsley. Sprinkle with red pepper to taste.

Lamb's Head / Kefalaki

No part of a lamb goes to waste by the Greeks. *Kefalaki riganato* or lamb's head oregano is considered one of the tastiest delicacies, a *meze* for *retsina* par excellence. Split the lamb's head in half and tie it back together with strings again to keep intact the brains. The head should be soaked for a while and cleaned until all the blood is gone. Then rub it with lemon juice, adding salt and pepper to the juice. You can either put the head as it is in a baking pan or remove the strings and put the two halves with the cut side up. Dilute some tomato sauce with water, add a teaspoon of oregano, chopped garlic, salt and pepper and pour it over the lamb's head. Use a fairly hot oven to bake and baste frequently until the meat is tender. Remove the brains, tongue and meat neatly from the bones with a sharp knife and serve on heated plate. Do not use too fat or too large heads because they are not tasty. Baby lamb's heads make a very popular appetizer too.

Shish Kebab / Souvlaki

1 leg of lamb (4-5 pounds), boned and cubed
2 medium onions
3 green peppers
1 teaspoon oregano
1/2 cup olive oil
3 bay leaves
6 tomatoes, quartered
2 garlic cloves, minced
juice of 2 lemons
1 cup white wine
salt and pepper

Shish kebab or *souvlaki* is very popular in Greek-American pic-nics.
Cut the onions and peppers into quarters, and cut each quarter in half. Combine all ingredients, except tomatoes, in a shallow roasting pan. Mix well so that meat is completely coated. Put in refrigerator for several hours. Before cooking, add tomatoes and mix well to coat with the juices. Place the meat cubes on skewers, alternating with green pepper slices, onion slices and tomato wedges. Lay the skewers in the pan with the marinade, turning several times. Place the skewered lamb on a rack, over the pan containing the marinade. Broil, turning several times and basting with marinade from the pan. Cook until the lamb is pink, about 25 minutes. *Souvlaki* goes with rice *pilafi*.

Lamb's "Sausage" / Kokoretsi

Kokoretsi, like *gyros* should be left for the experts. But, with a long spit and charcoal oven you can try your luck. You need the heart, liver, kidney, sweetbreads and intestines of a young lamb. As in *mayeritsa* soup, boil the meats, after you wash them very thoroughly—the intestines inside and out using a stick or a pensil. Cut the meats in thick pieces and impale them on the spit. Mould them into a fairly thick and long "sausage." Wind the meats with the intestines to keep them together and grill slowly. Baste from time to time with a sauce of olive oil and lemon juice highly seasoned with salt, pepper and oregano. Cut to slices the size of a donut and serve warm.
Kokoretsi makes a delicious *meze* like the *kefalaki* and *gyros*. They are all appetizers and by no means can be considered as main meat dishes.

Meat Stew / Kapama

2 pounds boneless beef, cubed	dash ground cloves
2 chopped onions	1 can tomato sauce (8-ounce)
2 cloves garlic, minced	1 can whole tomatoes (16-ounce)
2 bay leaves	1 cup white wine
1 cinnamon stick, cut in half	butter
dash ground cinnamon	salt and pepper

Kapama or stewed meat is a classic dish for the Greeks. The favorite is beef but lamb is also common. Season beef cubes with salt and pepper, 4 tablespoons melted butter, garlic and onion, and saute until brown. Add bay leaves, cinnamon, cloves, tomatoes, tomato sauce and wine. Stir well, cover and simmer over low fire about 1 hour or until lamb is tender. Stir occasionally and make sure that the sauce covers the meat, adding water or stock if necessary. *Kapama* goes well with macaroni. When beef is almost cooked, boil macaroni in salted water according to directions on the package. Drain macaroni and arrange half of it on a platter; sprinkle with grated cheese; cover with remaining macaroni; and top with more grated cheese. Melt 1/4 pound butter in a skillet until it turns golden brown; then pour butter and spoon pan sauce from *kapama* over the macaroni. Serve immediately.

Beef-Onion Stew / Stifatho

3 pounds stewing beef	1 glass red wine
3 pounds small onions	1/2 glass wine vinegar
1/2 cup olive oil	2 bay leaves
3 tomatoes (ripe) or	1 cinnamon stick
1 tablespoon	pinch of cumin
tomato paste	salt and pepper

This is properly the richest Greek dish, and a very popular one, especially in winter time. If you can get hold of a clay casserole it is the proper one to use for *stifatho*. Cut the beef in serving pieces and brown it lightly in half the olive oil in a saucepan. Then put it in the casserole and cover with hot water. Stew slowly for about an hour. Make a puree with the tomatoes, and add it to the meat with the remaining olive oil, wine and vinegar, garlic and other spices and the onions shelled but whole. Use a wooden spoon to stir once or twice and cover the casserole to cook very slowly for another two hours. Do not stir anymore in order not to break the onions. Instead, rock the casserole from time to time. Let the *stifatho* stand for awhile before serving. Veal makes tasty *stifatho* also.

Ground Beef and Macaroni Pie / Pasticcio II

2 pounds ground beef	1 8-ounce can tomato sauce
1 chopped onion	1/2 cup white wine
1 tablespoon chopped parsley	butter
1 garlic clove, minced	3 eggs, beaten
1 pound macaroni	grated cheese
1 teaspoon cinnamon	4 cups bechamel sauce
1/2 teaspoon nutmeg	salt and pepper

Pastitsio and *moussaka* are the two most popular, and richer appetizers.
Using a fork crumble the meat as you saute it until golden brown. Add 4 tablespoons of butter, the onions, garlic and parsley. Add cinnamon, nutmeg, salt, pepper, wine and tomato sauce; simmer for 30 minutes, and remove from the fire. In the meantime boil the macaroni in salted water, according to the directions on the package. When cooked, rinse and drain the macaroni; place it in a bowl, and add 1/4 pound melted butter, beaten eggs, and a generous sprinkling of grated cheese. Mix well and spread half of the macaroni mixture on the bottom of a greased baking pan, about 9x13x2 inches and cover evenly with the meat sauce. Sprinkle with grated cheese, spread remaining macaroni over meat, sprinkle with grated cheese, cover with bechamel sauce, sprinkle lavishly with grated cheese, dot with butter, and sprinkle very delicately with a few pinches of cinnamon. Bake at 350° for 1 hour. Cool and cut into desired size squares.

Meat-Rice Balls / Yuvarlakia

2 pounds hashed meat	3 teaspoon parsley
2 large onions	1 teaspoon mint
3 pounds rice	Egg-lemon sauce
2 ounces butter	salt and
1 tablespoon vinegar	pepper

In a mixing bowl put the hashed meat, onions, parsley, mint and half the butter and knead well until fully blended. Add the rice, after you scald it for five minutes, and continue to knead until you make an even mixture. Use vinegar and hot water to moisten, add salt and pepper and leave the mixture in a cool place for about half an hour. Then begin shaping the mixture into round balls the size of a golf ball and arrange them in a large saucepan. Pour enough boiling water to cover the meat balls but be careful to pour from the side of the saucepan to prevent breaking of the meat balls. Add salt and the remaining butter and cover with a pyrex plate. Simmer for 45 minutes to an hour. After you make an egg and lemon sauce (see recipe) with the broth from the pan, pour it over the meat balls and serve immediately.

Meat Pie / Kreatopitta

1-1/2 pound hashed beef or veal
2 onions not too large
2 pounds butter

1 pound f i l o
1/2 cup white sauce
2 tablespoons tomato juice
salt and pepper

First soften the onions after you chop them as finely as possible and boil them in a little water for five minutes. Add the hashed meat, tomato juice, butter and seasoning and stir well. Let simmer for about 15 minutes and add the white (bechamel) sauce, as indicated in the sauce recipe. Place five to six sheets of *filo* well oiled, on a baking tin, spread the filling evenly and cover with the the remaining *filo* sheets well oiled to keep smooth. Seal the filling by folding the edges and cut the surplus of the *filo* around the tin with a very sharp knife. Bake in a moderate oven until golden and crisp. It takes about an hour. For better flavor cover the tin with greaseproof paper. Cut in squares or any desired size to serve.

Jellied Pig / Pikti

3 pig's feet
1/2 pig's head
Juice of 3 lemons and 2 oranges

2 cloves garlic
1 bay leaf
6 peppercorns
salt and pepper

Boil salted water and cover the head and feet (cleansed thoroughly). Simmer gently until the meat begins to fall from the bones. Add the peppercorns and bay leaf. While the meat is cooling enough to handle, crush the garlic in a mortar and mix with lemon juice. Remove all the bones, cut the meat into small pieces and place them in a form. Add the garlic with lemon juice, the orange juice, pepper and a little more salt if you like. Pour from the liquid you cooked the pig's head and feet enough to cover the meat. Rock the form to distribute the liquid evenly and place the form in a cool place to jelly. You can decorate with olive oils and sliced celery and serve the same way as any jelly.

Meat Loaf / Roulo

>2 pounds chopped meat
>1 cup bread crumbs
>6 eggs
>1 cup tomato sauce
>3 tablespoons butter
>1 teaspoon sugar
>2 onions
>1/2 cup chopped parsley
>Salt and pepper

First add to the chopped meat one egg, raw the onions chopped and the parsley. Mix well, spread the meat mixture on a board, and place the five eggs, boiled, in a line, in the center. Fold the meat over and dust with flour or dry bread crumbs. Place the meat loaf in boiling butter and cook until golden brown on one side. Then turn over to brown the other side. You can also put the loaf in a baking dish and brown in a hot oven. Dilute a cup of tomato sauce with a cup of water and add a teaspoon of sugar. Pour over the *roulo* and bake for half an hour until the water is absorbed. Slice on a hot plate.

Liver With Sauce / Sikotakia Saltsa

Liver is usually fried. This recipe, for added flavor, includes a special way of cooking, used in many Greek islands. The liver should be calf's. Chop about half a pound and marinate in red wine for about an hour. Brown lightly two small sliced onions in a pan with four tablespoons of olive oil. Take the liver pieces from the wine and pat them dry. Coat them lightly in well-seasoned flour. Now brown the liver in the pan adding a little more olive oil if the onions have absorbed too much. Add a pinch of spices to the red wine and put in the liver and the onions as they get brown. Cook slowly until the liver is tender and the sauce thick. Use the sauce over mashed potatoes. It makes a very tasty dish.

Hare With Onions / Lagos Stifadho

3 pounds hare	1 teaspoon tomato paste
3 pounds small onions	4 cloves garlic
1/2 pint olive oil	2 bay leaves
1 wineglass red wine	1 cinnamon stick
1/2 wineglass wine vinegar	Salt and pepper

A very rich and popular dish. Should be cooked in casserole. Cut the hare into serving portions and brown lightly in a pan with half the olive oil before putting in the casserole.

Barely cover with hot water and stew gently for about 1 hour. Squeeze the tomatoes, add the onions, garlic bay leaves, spices and wine, vinegar and the remainder of the olive oil, mix and pour over the meat. Use a wooden spoon to stir, cover and cook very slowly for a further two hours. Rock the casserole now and then instead of stirring to help the onions remain whole. Keep out of the fire for awhile before serving. *Kouneli* (rabbit) can substitute for hare.

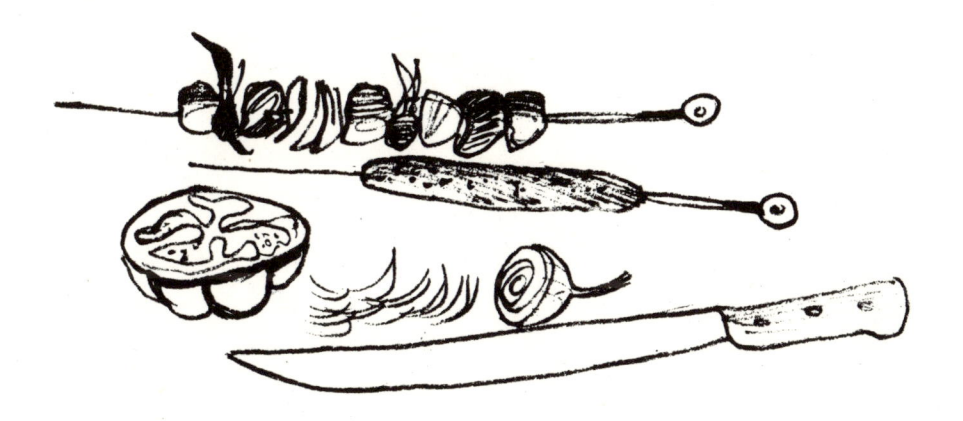

THOSE WONDERFUL FLYING CREATURES

*"Crito, I owe a cock to
Aesclepius; will you remember
to pay the debt?"*
    Socrates' last words

Greeks have a very popular maxim:

«῎Οπου λαλοῦν πολλοὶ κοκκόροι ἀργεῖ νὰ ξημερώση»

Which means "dawn comes late to the places where too many cocks warble." We, cooks, have just about the same maxim in saying "too many cooks spoil the broth." However, the point is that too many cocks warble in Greek countryside, apparently because too many cooks take away from the *kotetsi,* the household, too many chicken and eggs "to spoil the cricken-broth." And, as you very well know, a tall and proudly walking cock can take care of quite a number of chicken. Greeks call a *kokoras* every male who likes to take care of lots of females.

It seems ancient Greeks liked to eat roosters as much as they liked to bet on their fights. Although a Greek *odigos mageirikis,* a cooking guide hardly includes any recipe for rooster specialty, they do not fail to provide for the preparation of *ortikia* (quails), *trigonia* (turtle doves), *becatses* (woodcocks) and *perdikes* (partridges), which a decent hunter never fails to bring you on the 12th day not of Xmas, but of September—unless he keeps them in the freezer for Christmas.

Most of the migrating birds of Europe come September start for warmer places, and Greece is one of their "posting stages." They bring out the hunters by the thousands and one gets the impression of war going on in the countryside. Losses are always very heavy for those wonderful flying creatures and Athenaeus says this was so since time immemorial—long before gun-powder was found. Here is a quotation from Athenaeus *Deipnosophists*:

*"Then let us have a cock, a tender pigeon,
  A partridge, and a few such other things;
And if a hare should offer, then secure it."*

STUFFING

Greeks like their birds stuffed. Stuffing is prepared in many different ways and you can always improvise. We selected the three basic ways of making stuffing: with minced meat, chestnuts and rice. The posology is for 5-7 pounds of chicken or turkey.

Minced Meat

1 pound minced beef	1/4 cup tomato sauce
3/4 pound calf's liver	1 tablespoon sugar
Turkey or chicken giblets	1 tablespoon parsley
1 onion	Salt and pepper

Simmer gently the liver and giblets with enough water to cover them in a small pan for about fifteen minutes. Let them cool and take them out to cut finely and mix with the *kima,* the minced beef. Add the onion, chopped parsley, sugar and season. Moisten with tomato juice and stuff the bird before roasting. You can make gravy by using the broth.

Chestnut

1 1/2 pounds chestnuts	1 tablespoon sugar
1 onion	Cinnamon
1 pound minced beef	3 ounces pine nuts
1/4 cup tomato juice	3 ounces raisins
	Salt and pepper

Boil and peel the chestnuts, leaving them whole. Slice the onion finely and *saute* lightly in a little butter until soft but not coloured, then add the minced meat and cook for a few minutes until the meat has lost its raw look. Add the tomato juice, sugar, salt, pepper and a pinch of cinnamon. Stir for a few minutes over a low fire and mix in the chestnuts, pine nuts and raisins, preferably sultanas. Leave to cool awhile and stuff the bird before roasting.

Rice

1 cup rice	1 dessertspoon
1 tablespoon grated cheese	chopped walnuts
2 ounces butter	Salt and pepper

This stuffing is prepared in giblet broth. Boil the rice into it for five minutes, cut the giblets and add them to the rice with the grated cheese, *kefalotiri* or parmesan and the chopped walnuts. Add the butter and a little water if necessary. Season and cook until the liquid is fully absorbed. Let it cool before stuffing the bird.

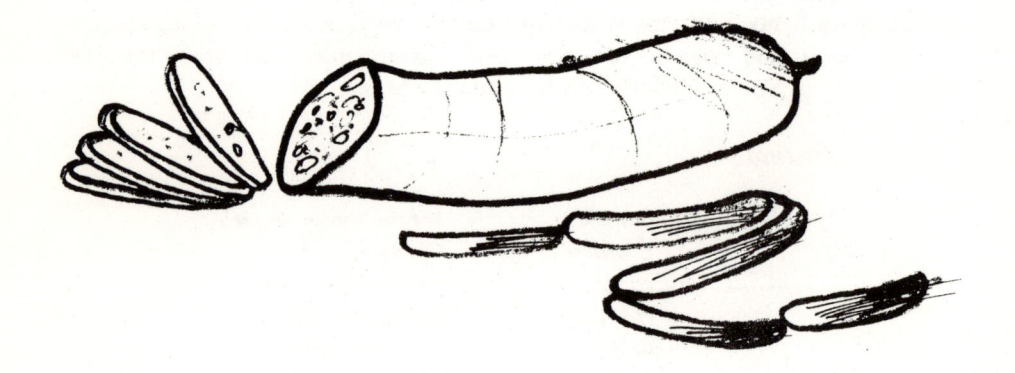

Chicken Pilaf / Kotopoulo Pilafi

1 chicken
3 tablespoons butter
1 cup chopped onions
1 can tomatoes
1 cup rice
Salt and pepper

Choose a medium size chicken. Cut it into serving pieces, place it in a saucepan with three tablespoons butter or fat and the onions. Simmer until golden brown, stirring occasionally. Add the canned tomatoes, cut in pieces and season. Cover and cook until the chicken is tender. Remove the bones from the chicken and have the *pilafi* ready as previously indicated.
Serve the rice in a platter surrounded with chicken, pour over the tomato sauce. Garnish with peas and serve hot.

Chicken With Noodles / Kotopoulo Me Hilopites

2 young chicken
3 ounces butter
1 pound noodles
2 onions
2 garlic cloves
6 tomatoes
1/2 cup tomato paste
1 cup dry white wine
4 stalks celery
3 tablespoons parsley
Grated cheese
Cinnamon, salt and pepper

Cut the chicken into serving pieces and rub them with salt and pepper. Brown them in hot butter and take them out of the pan. Keep them hot. Chop the onions finely and pound the garlic cloves and cook in the fat for awhile until they change color. Add the chicken pieces and pour the wine. Simmer for about fifteen minutes. Peel and chop the tomatoes and add them with the paste. Add the celery and parsley finely chopped, season and pour enough water to cover. Simmer until the chicken is very tender. In the meantime prepare the sauce in another pan. Place the noodles in boiling water and cook until tender. About the time the chicken starts to become soft add a pinch of cinnamon—not sooner. Take the chicken out of the pan and keep hot. Work with the sauce and the noodles after you drain the water. Add the sauce and alternate with grated cheese. Serve separately and have additional grated cheese to garnish as everyone likes.

Chicken Stew / Kotopoulo Kapama

1 chicken	1 lemon
6 tomatoes	3 ounces olive oil
2 tablespoons tomato paste	Cinnamon
3 ounces butter	Salt and pepper

Mix the lemon juice with half teaspoon of cinnamon, salt and pepper and rub the pieces of the chicken well. Heat the butter and olive oil together and brown the pieces of chicken. Take the chicken out and keep them hot. Peel and chop the tomatoes and add them with the tomato paste and a cup of hot water to the pan with the butter and olive oil. Stir well and cook until the tomatoes are very soft. Then return the pieces of chicken to the pan, coat them well with the sauce, cover and cook until the chicken meat is soft and ready to fall off the bone.

Grilled Chicken / Kotopoulo Tis Sharas

2 broiler chickens	Lemon
Olive oil	Garlic
1/2 teaspoon dry mustard	Salt and pepper

Split the chickens in two and rub the pieces well with a mixture of lemon juice, olive oil, salt and pepper and then with a peeled garlic clove. The same mixture with mustard will make the sauce. Cook the sauce for about three minutes stirring continually. Have the chicken placed in a shallow pan and grill until are brown and tender. Baste frequently with the sauce. Select young and plumb chicken and after you rub them leave them for about an hour while making the sauce. If you use a revolving spit baste the chicken frequently with the sauce. Grill in very low heat otherwise the chicken will burn.

Chicken Fricasse / Kotopoulo Fricasse

1 chicken	1/2 cup parsley
2 eggs	1 cup milk
1 lemon	2 tablespoons butter
1/4 cup olive oil	2 tablespoons flour
1 garlic clove	Salt and pepper

First chop and brown the garlic in hot olive oil. Cut the chicken into serving pieces and brown it. Season with salt and pepper, add water, cover the pan and cook until tender. In the meantime prepare the sauce. Melt the butter, add the flour and cream and mix them well stirring constantly until even. Add the parsley finely chopped and bring to boil. Beat the egg yolks with lemon juice and work with the cream sauce gradually blending into the egg mixture. Finally pour the egg mixture into the cream sauce, add salt, and cook over low heat for about three minutes stirring constantly. Then pour the sauce over the cooked chicken and take it out of the fire. Let it settle a little before serving.

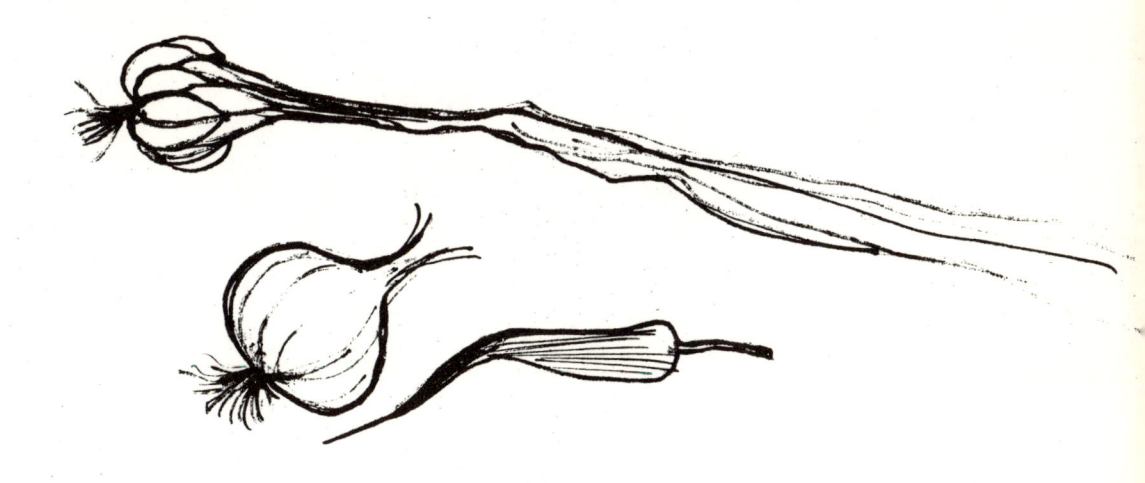

Roast Chicken Oregano / Kotopoulo Riganato

1 large broiler or fryer chicken	1 lemon
2 ounces butter	1/4 teaspoon oregano
2 ounces olive oil	Salt and pepper

First rub the chicken with a mixture of lemon juice, salt and pepper. Let it settle for about an hour and then put it in a pan with the olive oil, melted butter and two cups of hot water. Place the bird lying on its back. Sprinkle with *rigani* and cook in a moderate oven, basting the chicken frequently, until very tender. Turn the chicken from time to time to avoid its sticking to the pan.

Stuffed Chicken / Kotopoulo Gemisto

1 large or two small chickens
1 cup diced white bread
1 cup finely chopped onions
6 slices bacon
Chicken giblets
Oregano
Salt and pepper

Singe and wash the chicken and prepare the stuffing. Chop up the giblets with three slices of bacon and mix together with the finely chopped onions and diced bread. Add seasoning and a pinch of *rigani*.
Stuff the bird with this dry stuffing. Butter it well on the outside and roast in the oven. Twenty minutes before removing from the oven, cover the breast with the rest of the bacon.

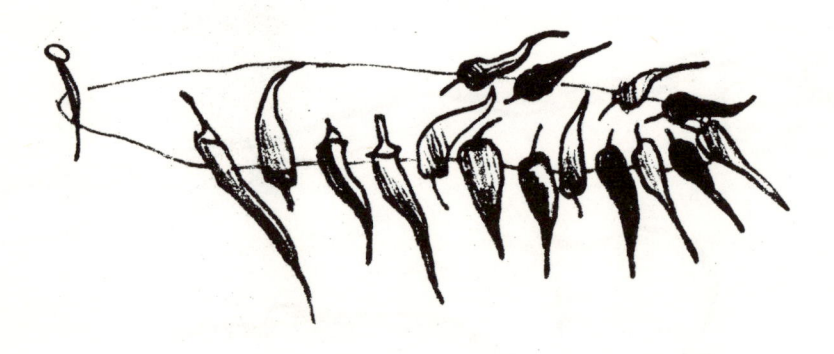

Chicken With Yoghourt / Kotopoulo Me Yaourti

1 medium-sized chicken
2 onions
1 tablespoon butter
1 tablespoon flour
1 cup yoghourt
Salt and pepper

Cut the chicken into serving pieces and fry in butter or fat until golden brown. Place the chicken in a saucepan, add chopped onion, salt and pepper and enough water to half cover the chicken. Cover the pan and simmer until tender. Mix the flour with a little water, add to the yoghourt, and pour over the chicken. Stir well until the sauce is perfectly smooth. Simmer for another ten minutes and serve hot.

Chicken Pie/Kotopitta

1 chicken	2 tablespoons grated cheese
12 ounces *filo*	3 tablespoons flour
3 eggs	Nutmeg
4 ounces butter	Salt and pepper

First, cover the chicken with cold water, season with salt and bring to the boil. Remove any scum that rises to the surface and simmer gently until cooked. Leave the bird in the broth, and when cool enough to handle, remove the meat from the bones and flake it finely with the fingers, discarding the skin and any hard pieces. Make a sauce with two ounces of butter, flour and the chicken broth. Add the eggs, well-beaten, and the grated cheese and pour over the chicken. Season to taste. Line a shallow baking-tin with half the *filo*, brushing each sheet with melted butter. Spread the filling evenly and cover with the remaining buttered pastry sheets. Fold in the ends neatly to seal in the filling and brush the top sheet liberally with butter. Score into squares with a sharp knife, cover with greaseproof paper and bake in a moderate oven for one hour or until golden and crisp. *Kotopitta* if cut into small pieces can be served as a *meze*. It is highly appreciated.

Stuffed Turkey/Galopoula Gemisti

1 medium-size turkey	1 cup butter
1 pound chopped meat	1 cup seedless raisins
3 onions	1 tablespoon pine nuts
1 pound tomatoes	1 tablespoon chopped parsley
2 cups bread crumbs	Salt and pepper

This is the traditional Thanksgiving dish. The Greeks prepare it for Christmas dinner. The stuffing is prepared in the usual manner with the ingredients indicated above. Sprinkle the turkey with salt and stuff the body, breast and neck opening of the turkey. Sew securely and rub the outside of the turkey with butter. Bake in a moderate oven for about three hours, depending on the size of the turkey. When the turkey is cooked, brown the chopped turkey liver lightly for a few minutes, add two tablespoons of flour, three cups of stock and simmer for about five minutes until blended. This makes a gravy to be served hot on the side, in a gravy boat.

"DIANA'S FORESTERS"

Let us be Diana's foresters,
gentlemen of the shade,
minions of the moon
Shakespeare : *King Henry IV,*
      Part I, ii 28

Greeks have a unique legacy in hunting. Since early times they were "Diana's foresters," especially in my birthplace, Nestani. Mount Artemission was nearby and, of course, a favored hunting spot. Up there, Artemis or Diana or Cynthia, the goddess of hunting lived.

"She was the Lady of Wild Things, Huntsman-in-chief to the gods, an odd office for a woman. Like a good huntsman, she was careful to preserve the young : she was "the protectress of dewy youth everywhere," so says Edith Hamilton in her mythology.

And that is why youth comes to Dianna's Opaa. They come to pay tribute to Artemis "the lover of woods and the wild chase over the mountain." And they feel secure and happy under her protection, like the hunters of antiquity, who build the Temple of Artemis in Ephesus, one of the seven wonders of the world.

Early in September the "hunters" rush by the thousands to the marshes and the lakes of Greece to meet the "clouds of migrating birds on their way south."

Many of these birds are tough or hard to cook but others are considered as great delicacies by the hunters. In the recipes that follow we take it for granted that you either buy the birds cleaned at the food Super Market of specialized meat shop or the housewife or cook knows how to clean and prepare it for cooking. Otherwise it is advisable to skip this chapter because cooking the wild feathered creatures in the Greek manner is a very complicated operation indeed.

Quail With Rice / Ortikia Pilafi

8 quail	1 tablespoon olive oil
1 glass red or white wine	1 cup rice
2 ounces butter	Salt and pepper

Use a *tsoukali*, an earthenware or pottery shallow casserole in cooking game birds. Place the *ortikia* with the butter, olive oil, wine and half a cup of water, season and cover. Cook for about an hour and a half, until the meat is ready to separate from the birds. Add the rice and simmer until soft, adding a little more water if needed.

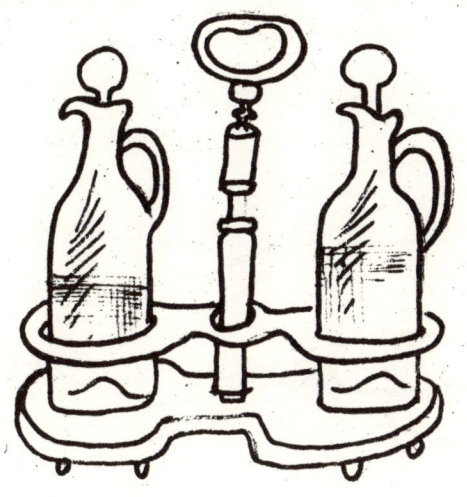

Grilled Quail / Ortikia Sharas

8 quail	Oregano
Olive oil	Salt and
Lemon juice	pepper

The simplest and easiest way to prepare *ortikia* is either grilled or on the spit. Hunters, after cleaning the birds, cut them in two, rub them with salt and pepper, roll them in a mixture of olive oil and oregano, let them marinade for about half an hour, turning them frequently, and then cook them under the grill or over a charcoal fire.

If they have a spit available, they thread the birds on to it and cook them over a high charcoal fire. They brush them frequently with olive oil and lemon juice to keep them moist and they turn them all the time as they cook.

As a youngster, I loved to go hunting with my parents and brothers and enjoyed immensely our life during the hunting season out in the woods. Wild birds, hares and rabbits were our delicious daily menu.

Partridges Salmi / Perdikes Salmi

4 partridges *1 lemon*
1/2 cup white wine *4 ounces butter*

First heat the butter in a frying pan. Take out the livers from the birds and save them. Put the birds in the butter and brown them well on all sides. Transfer to a pot. Cut the livers and brown them. Pour the wine into the pan with the butter; stir to loosen all the particles stuck to the pan, add the lemon juice and a cup of hot water. Mix well and pour over the birds. Cover the pot, and simmer, adding a little more water, if needed. Cook about 1 1/2 hours until the meat separates easily from the bones.

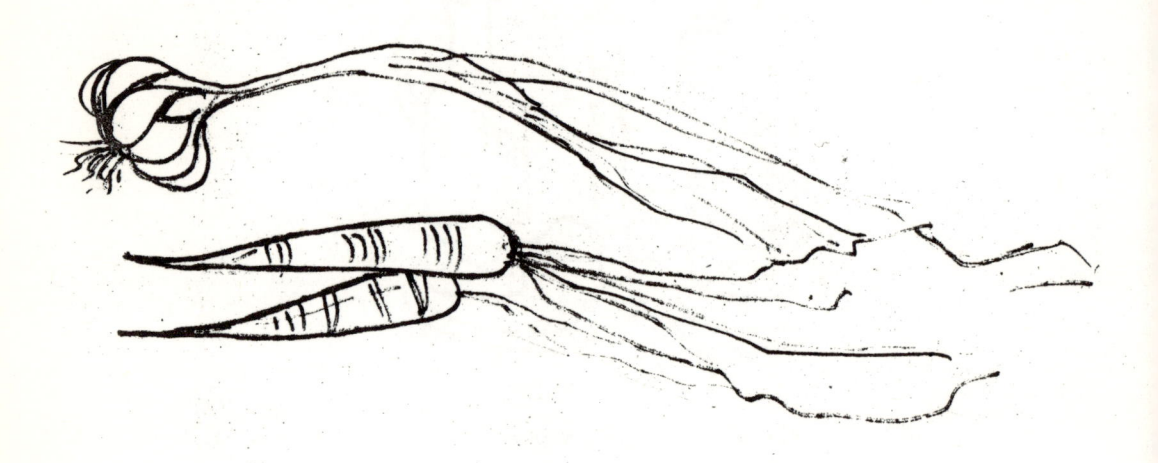

Partridges With Olives / Perdikes Me Elies

4 partridges *3 ounces butter*
4 tomatoes *1 tablespoon*
2 heads celery *olive oil*
3 ounces olives *Salt and pepper*

Select the green stoned Greek olives. Most Greek groceries have them. Place them in a pan and let them simmer for about ten minutes in their own juices. Clean the celery and chop it into small pieces. Heat enough butter to fry the partridges until brown, then add the celery and the olives, the tomatoes and enough water to just cover. Add salt and cook until tender. Cut the birds into halves, arrange on a platter and pour the sauce over them. Out of this world...

Pigeons Tomato Sauce / Pitsounia Yahni

4-6 pigeons
1 cup white wine
2 pounds tomatoes

4 ounces olive oil
Salt and pepper

First season the *pitsounia* lightly with salt and pepper. Heat the olive oil in a frying pan, and add the birds. Brown them well on all sides and transfer to a pot. Add the wine and the tomatoes, peeled and strained, to the oil and cook for about five minutes. Pour the sauce over the birds. Add the water, cover the pot and simmer until tender. The birds are done when their meat separates easily from the bones. Add a little more water, if needed, during the cooking. The sauce will thicken during the cooking, making a delicious *yahni* dish.

THOSE MARVELOUS SWIMMERS

A piece of a broiled fish,
and of a honeycomb
St. Luke, XXIV 42

When a Greek wonderer to foreign lands sails back home his first thought is to lite a candle to Virgin Mary's ikon and give thanks for his safe arrival. Next is to have some fish—any kind of fish. Because, for a Greek, no fish tastes like a Greek fish.

Greece is surrounded by water. Practically every other town is a seaport. There are thousands upon thousands of islands in Greece's Mediterranean waters. And if you tell a Greek he should eat fish every Friday he will look at you, smile, and agree wholeheartedly: "Good, then let's call everyday a Friday," he will simply say. And, indeed, there is no Greek restaurant without a daily menu including a variety of fish.

Greek hunters of the antiquity may have had a great protector in goddess Diana, but fishermen had Poseidon, Neptune, Lord and Ruler of the sea, second in emminence only to Zeus himself, an almighty god, who could shatter whatever he pleased with his *triaina*, the three-pronged spear that could thunder the waves and sink them into stillness at will.

"Lord Poseidon, from you this pride is ours"

Greek seamen worshipped him on both sides of the Aegean and to him they devoted the splendid temple on top of Sounion.
Every Greek, whether a fisherman or not, is an *Argonaut*. Sooner or later he will have to pass through the *Symplegades* of life, through the Clashing Rocks that "roll perpetually against one another while the sea boils up around them." They should know how and when to send the Dove of Hope to pass through the *Symplegades* and turn back without being crushed. Greeks proved their superiority as *Argonauts* since time immemorial and one only has to read the tales of Creation by Hesiod or their classical mythology and the Homeric songs to marvel. Aristotle's essay on the life of the natives of the sea is as important as his *Politics*. Perhaps the only contrast between these two masterpieces is that while in *Politics* Aristotle maintains that the State ought to be small enough so that each citizen should be able to know every other citizen by sight, in his *Peri Ihthyon* treatise he recognizes this cannot be the case "on the deep."

The wealth of the sea is immense. No one can give you a complete guide to cooking the innumerable varieties of fish and shellfish. Yet, no one is better qualified to get you acquainted with a few dozen of well-known varieties of those marvelous swimmers than a Greek housewife. Boy, how she knows the fish... She can recognize *achinoi*, the sea urchins and select the females at their best and sweetest, and that is at full moon. She has learned how to avoid the quite black, rather smaller male *achinos* with the longer and sharper spikes and concentrate on the purple females, who like to adorn themselves with tiny pebbles or strands of seaweed. And she knows how to grasp them firmly in her hand and prise them away from the rocks to which they cling, avoiding even a pinch of their spines. She will cut a large hole in their flat head with a knife and carefully remove the coral from the sides with a teaspoon to serve it as an appetizer on a small dish with olive oil and a little lemon juice. Unless you like to sip them from the shell like the oysters.

Every housewife knows how to boil, fry or grill her fish. My recipes, therefore, will concentrate particularly with doing something else with a fish—the Greek way. As long as you send the fish to the table complete with the head, which is considered by the Greek as the best part, the recipes apply to any of many varieties, unless otherwise specified. Fishhouses, as a rule, have an expert to tell you which fish is best to boil, bake or fry. And, as a general advice, the Greeks prefer their fish grilled, baked and fried—in that order.

Boiled Fish / Psari Vrasto

           3 pounds fish   6 carrots
           1 pound onions   10 potatoes
           1/4 cup olive oil   1 tablespoon chopped dill
           1 bunch celery   Salt and pepper

First put the vegetables to boil in a fish kettle with about three quarters of water. The kettle or pan should be big enough to take the whole fish. Select any type og boiling fish about three pounds. Also be careful to select small, young and fresh vegetables. Add the olive oil and dill to the vegetables and season. Have the fish ready to place it in the pan when the vegetables are partly cooked. Simmer until the fish is tender. If the vegetables are ready before the fish, lift them from the pan and keep them warm. You can either garnish with the vegetables and serve an olive and lemon sauce or you can turn the broth into an *avgolemono* soup and serve as a first course. For more instruction consult *psarosoupa*.

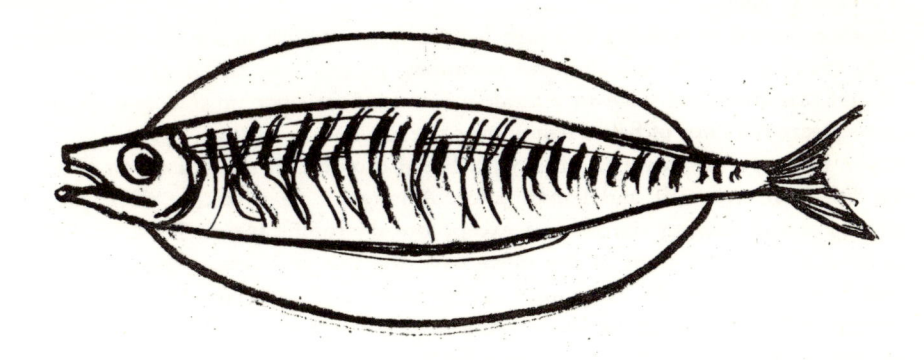

Broiled Fish / Psari Sharas

           3 pounds fish   1/2 cup olive oil
           2 lemons   Oregano, salt and pepper

Small whole fish, trout or any other kind of less than a pound each are the best to be broiled. Always select your fish carefully. If the fish looks at you with a clear bright eye it tells you "I'm O.K." Clean the inside, wash well and sprinkle it inside and out with lemon juice, salt and pepper. Let it settle for half an hour, drain and broil at low oven for about forty minutes. Turn it occasionally very carefully to avoid breaking. Make a sauce with 3/4 of a cup lemon juice and half a cup of olive oil. Beat until light and fluffy. Pour over the fish and let it stand ten minutes before serving, but keep warm. Sprinkle with *rigani*. Always use the best quality of pure olive oil whenever you cook fish.

Fish Spetsiota / Psari Spetsiota

3 pounds white fish	1 teaspoon sugar
3 tomatoes	1 lemon
3 tablespoons olive oil	1/4 glass white wine
1 tablespoon parsley	1 cup bread crumbs
6 garlic cloves	Salt and pepper

Spetsiota is the most popular fish dish in Greece and can be prepared in many different ways. This is the original and authentic way. You can use any whole fish, or fish steaks, or even dried cod, which it should be cut into serving portions and soaked overnight. You should change the water a couple of times. First, skin and chop the tomatoes and put them into a pan with the olive oil and half a cup of water. Add the chopped parsley, sliced garlic and a teaspoon of sugar. Season and cook for fifteen minutes. Lower the fish carefully into the pan and poach gently in the sauce until the fish is cooked. Allow to stand for half an hour. To serve, put the fish on a large dish and pour the sauce over it. It is equally good eaten hot or cold.

Another method of cooking this dish is to arrange the fish in a well-oiled baking-dish, smother it with the chopped tomatoes, parsley and sliced garlic, add the oil and seasoning and bake in a moderate oven. Serve hot or cold and in either case squeeze the juice of half a lemon over the fish before serving.

If you like, you can cover the fish with bread crumbs. In such case you first rub the fish well with salt and lemon juice. Arrange it in a baking dish, put the oil and the remaining ingredients except bread crumbs into a bowl and blend as for a sauce. Pour most of the sauce over the fish and cover with half of the bread crumbs. Take the remainder of the sauce and pour this over the bread-crumbs. Add the remaining bread crumbs to make a top layer. This is done to produce a thick crust. Bake for about an hour in a moderate oven, basting the fish from time to time in its own sauce. If the fish should seem too dry, add some hot water, or, better still, white wine, but only a little sauce should be left by the time the fish is ready. Fish *Spetsiota* actually is another way of making *plaki*.

Stewed Fish / Psari Plaki

2 pounds fish	1 cup tomato sauce, or
1/2 pound onions	1 pound tomatoes
1 glass white wine	1 tablespoon bread crumbs
2 tablespoons parsley	Olive oil, salt and pepper

Use large fish sliced to steaks. Chop the onions and fry them in olive oil, until golden brown. Add wine, salt, pepper, the fish and a small glass of water. Add tomato sauce diluted with a little water or place a slice of fresh tomato on each slice of fish. Sprinkle with chopped parsley, bread crumbs and a little more salt. Cover and let simmer for half an hour. If you like you can add a sliced garlic clove. In such case squeeze in the juice of a lemon and rock the pan to distribute it evenly. Be careful not to break the fish steaks and serve with the tomato on top.

Fish With Lemon / Psari Lemonato

3 pounds fish	1 lemon
1 onion	1 tablespoon parsley
1 teaspoon *rigani*	1/4 cup olive oil
1 garlic clove	Salt and pepper

First make a mixture of salt and pepper and rub the fish. Put it in an oiled baking plate. Spread the onion and garlic on top of the fish and sprinkle with either *rigani* or parsley (do not use them both). Pour the olive oil and lemon juice over it and leave to marinate for an hour. Bake in a moderate oven for forty-five minutes, basting from time to time. You can skip the onion and garlic, if you do not like them. It tastes just as good.

Fish Wine Sauce / Psari Krasato

3 pounds fish	2 teaspoons
2 cups white wine	mustard
Olive oil	Salt and pepper

Have the fish cleaned inside but do not remove the head and tails. Place it in an oiled pan after you rub the cleaned inside and out with salt and pepper. Add the wine and two cups of lukewarm water and mix the mustard in it. Bake in moderate oven until tender. Baste from time to time. Add more wine not water, if the sauce is reduced too much during the cooking. Make two or three incisions to the skin of the fish to keep it from bursting.

Fish Marine / Psari Marinato

2 pounds fish	1 teaspoon rosemary
1 cup oil	1 teaspoon sugar
1/2 cup tomato sauce	3 cloves crushed garlic
1/2 cup vinegar	
4 tablespoons flour	Salt and pepper

You can use either one whole fish or fish steaks. First heat half of the oil in a frying pan to a high temperature. Dust the fish with flour and fry, a few at a time, until golden brown. Strain the oil into a cup and clean the pan with absorbent paper. Pour the oil into it again and, if necessary, add a little more oil. Heat it again and add the flour, stirring with a spoon to a light brown color. Add the vinegar, water, tomato sauce, sugar, salt, pepper and the crushed garlic. Stir with a wire whisk until smooth, and simmer for fifteen minutes. Add the rosemary, stir, and pour the sauce immediately on the fish, lined on a deep platter. Let it settle and always serve cool.

Fish Savoury / Psari Savoro

4 pounds fish	3 garlic cloves
1 cup tomato sauce	Olive oil
3 tablespoons white wine	Bayleaves and rosemary
1 ounce flour	Salt and pepper

Red snapper or mullet is the best for *savoro*. Actually *savoro* is a variation of the *marinato* with tomato sauce added. First fry the fish in hot oil until brown on both sides. Put the fish into a deep serving dish. Throw out the oil, keeping about a tablespoon of it. Reheat in the pan, add the flour and stir. Add the tomato sauce, wine, finely chopped garlic, a little rosemary and a couple of bayleaves. Simmer the sauce for five minutes, then pour it over the fish. Let it cool before serving.

Trout Oregano / Pestrofa Riganati

2 large trouts	4 ounces butter
2 lemons	Oregano, salt and pepper

Cut the fish into filets and place it in a broiler pan. Salt and pepper should be added on the meaty side only. Squeeze the juice of one lemon over it, dot with butter and sprinkle with *rigani*. Put to broil in a moderate, 400°, flame until it browns lightly. From time to time baste with the juice, adding more lemon juice and butter, if needed. When cooked, place in hot platter, add the remaining butter, sprinkle with more *rigani* and serve hot. Garnish with lemon slices.

Porgies With Celery/*Tsipoura Selino*

3 pounds porgies	1 cup olive oil
4 pounds celery	2 eggs
1 onion	2 lemons, salt and pepper

First clean, cut into pieces and cook for about five minutes the celery in boiling water. Drain and keep aside. Chop the onion and cook it soft in the oil. Add a cup of water and when it is brought to boil throw the celery in and simmer until tender. Have the porgies prepared. Lay them on top of the celery. Add a little salt, pepper, and water, if needed. Cover and simmer for about twenty minutes. Beat the eggs well with the lemon juice adding gradually some of the liquid from the pot. Beat constantly. When well blended, pour the sauce back into the pot, shake the pot gently and continue to simmer over low heat until the sauce thickens.

Fish Mayonnaise, Athenian Style/ *Athinaiki Mayoneza*

3 pounds white fish	2 celery leaves
2 onions	1 egg
2 carrots	1 lemon
2 tomatoes	Salt and pepper

This is a must dish for all Athenian restaurants and a delicious one, depending on the quality of the fish and of the mayonnaise. First you boil the fish adding to the water the onions, carrots, celery, and tomatoes. The broth, strained, can be served as a *psarosoupa*, in which case you flavor it with a beaten egg and lemon (see *avgolemono* soup). The fish should be boned and broken into small pieces, with all the skin removed. Place the pieces into a cup, reverse it on a plate and cover with mayonnaise. Garnish with green olives cut in half, *kapari*, slices of fresh cucumber and pickles and serve. It makes an outstanding summer dish.

Swordfish On Skewer / Ksifias Souvlaki

2 pounds swordfish
1 tablespoon oil
1 tablespoon parsley
1 lemon
Bay leaves
Salt and pepper

Mix oil, salt, pepper and chopped parsley in a bowl and dip the fish in it. Cut the sword fish in pieces the size of a walnut. Pass 5-6 pieces of fish through a skewer with a bay leaf in between each piece. Broil until tender and serve with oil and lemon sauce.

This is the famous Stelios' recipe, for his popular *fisheria* in Alimos, close to the Athens' airport.

Boiled Codfish / Bakaliaros Vrastos

2 pounds codfish
10 onions
2 pounds potatoes
4 sticks celery
1/2 cup olive oil
1 lemon, pepper

If you use dried or salt codfish you should soak it overnight, changing the water at lest a couple of times. Always select small vegetables and peel them. Remove the skin of the codfish, drain and put into a pan with the onions, chopped celery and potatoes. Cover with water. Beat the olive oil, lemon juice and pepper add and stir. Simmer until the fish is tender. Serve with the vegetables and an oil and lemon dressing. Dried codfish is usually served with *skordalia* sauce, but in such case the preparation is somehow different.

Codfish Garlic Sauce / Bakaliaros Skordalia

3 pounds codfish
1 teaspoon olive oil
Skordalia sauce
1/2 teaspoon baking soda
6 ounces flour
Pepper

This is a very popular fish dish. Have your sweetheart eat it too if a kiss is included in your evening's menu. Soak overnight the fish if you use dried one. Cut it into serving portions and change the water a couple of times. Dry the pieces well before frying. Make a fairly thick flour and water batter, seasoned with pepper. Just before using add the olive oil and baking soda. Dip each piece of fish into the batter and fry until crisp and golden in a deep pan of very hot olive oil. Pile on a serving dish and serve with a bowl of *skordalia* sauce. See the recipe in sauces.

Scallops With Rice / Htenia Pilafi

2 pounds scallops
1-1/2 cup rice
3/4 cup olive oil
1/3 cup of butter
1 onion
Salt and pepper

This is rather a Greek-American dish, since scallops are practically unknown in Greece. Slice the onion finely and fry it in olive oil until golden brown. Add the scallops well cleaned, cover and cook for about half an hour. Stir from time to time. Wash the rice thoroughly and place in bowl with salt and hot water, soak for half an hour and drain well. Roll in dish towel and let stand for another fifteen minutes. Then put the rice in a skillet, add butter and fry for ten minutes, stirring constantly. Add the rice and a little water, if needed, cover, and reduce heat to cook for ten minutes on low. Keep covered after the rice has been added to avoid scorching, and rock the sauce pan with both hands several times. When done, stir and let stand ten minutes to settle.

Shrimps With Rice / Garides Pilafi

2 pounds shrimps
1 can tomatoes
1-1/2 cup rice
2 onions
1/2 cup olive oil
1/2 butter
Salt and pepper

When making *pilafi* use the best quality of long grain rice and pure olive oil. First chop the onions and saute in olive oil until golden brown. Add the tomatoes, stir and cook, covered for about five minutes. Have the shrimps washed thoroughly and shelled. Add them to the sauce and cook for about five minutes after you season, stir well and cover. Remove them from the fire and prepare the rice as directed in the previous recipe. When you put the rice into the pan, add butter and cook for ten minutes on low fire, stirring constantly. Keep covered after rice has been added and rock the pan several times during cooking. Allow to stand ten minutes before serving.

Fried Shrimps / Garides Tiganites

2 pounds shrimps *2 eggs, olive oil*
4 ounces flour *Nutmeg, salt and pepper*

Fresh shrimps keep their delicate flavor better and should always be preferred to frozen ones. After you wash them well—no matter if they are fresh or frozen—and remove all sand or dirt, put them in a pan without water and let them simmer in their own liquid for ten minutes. Shake the pan from time to time to make sure they are cooked evenly. Let them cool and shell them. Prepare a batter with the flour and eggs yolks, thinning down to the required consistency with water. Add the olive oil and seasoning. Beat the egg whites until they form peaks and fold into the batter. Coat each shrimp with the batter, drop into a deep pan of very hot olive oil and fry until crisp and golden. Drain on a sheet of greaseproof paper and serve at once with a mayonnaise sauce.

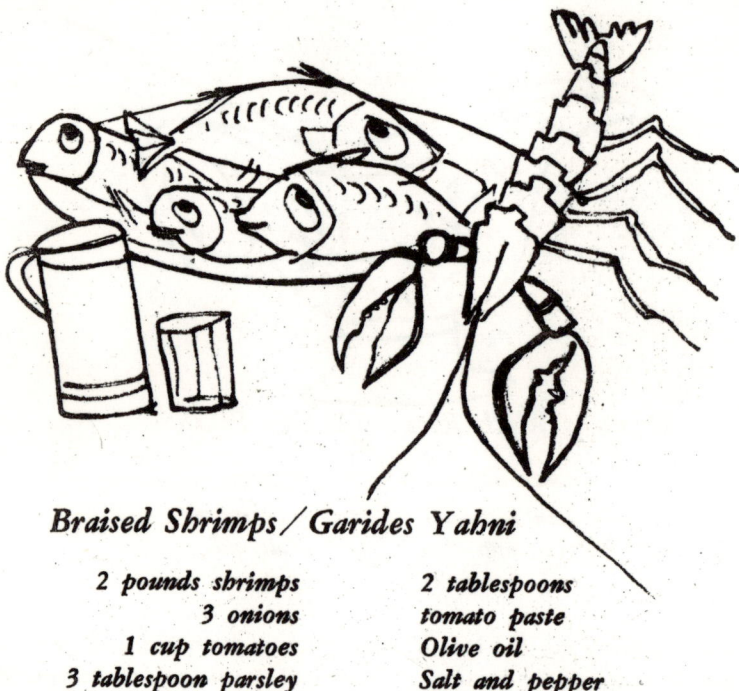

Braised Shrimps / Garides Yahni

2 pounds shrimps *2 tablespoons*
3 onions *tomato paste*
1 cup tomatoes *Olive oil*
3 tablespoon parsley *Salt and pepper*

Chop the onions and saute with olive oil until golden brown. Add the tomato paste and the tomatoes, crushed. Cook three minutes and add the parsley, chopped. Cook three more minutes and add the shrimps after you wash and drain well. Leave them unshelled. Season, cover and cook until the shrimps are tender enough to be removed from the shell easily. *Garides yahni* should not be let to cool. Serve immediately.

Fried Squids / Kalamaria Tiganita

3 pounds squids *1 lemon, olive oil*
4 ounces flour *Salt and pepper*

Greeks love very tiny squids as a delicacy. They make a most appreciated *meze* because they are sweet and tender and can be fried as a whole. When very large *kalamaria* should be used either for *pilafi* or to be stuffed. After you wash them well and drain, dust into the flour and season. Fry in very hot olive oil until crisp and golden brown. Serve immediately with a squeeze of lemon juice.

Squids With Rice / Kalamaria Pilafi

2 pounds squids *3/4 cup olive oil*
1 onion *1 can tomatoes*
2 cups rice *2 ounces butter*

First remove ink sac and bones from squid, wash thoroughly, cut the heads and entrails from body and cut into tiny pieces. Heat the butter and saute for ten minutes. Remove the liquid from the squids and save for use later. Add the chopped onion and cook for fifteen minutes. Strain the tomatoes and add them with the liquid from the squids. Season, bring to a boil and cover. Cook over medium flame until the squids are tender. Prepare the rice with butter as for *pilafi* and pour it in the pan, adding water if needed. Cook over low flame for ten more minutes and serve immediately.

Stuffed Squids / Kalamaria Gemista

5 pounds squids
2 onions
1/2 cup rice
3/4 cup olive oil

2 tablespoons tomato paste
1 cup canned tomatoes
2 tablespoons mint
Salt and pepper

Remove first the ink sac and bones from the squids. Wash thoroughly and cut the heads and entrails. Cut the feelers from heads and with entrails chop them fine on a board and place in a bowl. Add the rice, half a cup of olive oil, finely chopped mint, tomato paste, tomatoes, salt and pepper to taste and mix well. Stuff the squids and replace the heads to keep the filling inside. Place in a baking dish and pour the remaining juice from the stuffing over the squids. Add the rest of the olive oil and water and bake in hot oven for twenty minutes and then simmer until the rice is tender. From time to time baste with the sauce. Serve immediately.

Lobster Mayonnaise / Astakos Mayoneza

Lobster
Vinegar

Parsley
Mayonnaise, salt

A small lobster, live, per person should be enough. First plunge lobsters heads first into boiling salted water adding a little vinegar for flavor. Cook swiftly for five minutes and continue for another ten simmering. Transfer them to cold water for fifteen minutes and dry with a cloth. Break the claws off and carefully cut the lobsters lengthwise. Lift the meat from the tail, cut into thick pieces, crack the claws and take out the meat. Arrange on a platter with the tail meat. Take out the coral and the green liver and mix with the mayonnaise. You can substitute mayonnaise with olive oil and lemon dressing.

Octopus In Wine / Htapodi Krasato

1 or 2 octopus	1 dessertspoon
1/2 cup olive oil	tomato paste
1-1/2 pound onions	2 garlic cloves
1-1/2 pound potatoes	1 glass red wine
2 bay leaves	Salt and pepper

Use one or two octopus depending on size. Wash them well and after you remove the ink and save it, cut the octopus into pieces about two inches long and put in a pan without water. Leave over a low fire for about twenty minutes until the juices have run out and evaporated. Shake the pan from time to time to avoid burning. Add the olive oil, onions, bay leaves, garlic and tomato paste diluted with a little water and stir for five minutes. Next put in the wine, the ink from the octopus and enough water just to cover the contents of the pan. Season and cook very slowly for an hour and a half, when the octopus should be tender. Half an hour before serving put in the potatoes and add a little more wine and water if necessary. Potatoes are optional in this dish.

Octopus With Rice / Htapodi Pilafi II

1 octopus	2 tomatoes
1 onion	1 dessertspoon
1/4 cup olive oil	tomato paste
6 ounces rice	Salt and pepper

Prepare the octopus as in the previous recipe. When the liquid has been absorbed add to the pan the finely chopped onion and olive oil and cook gently for fifteen minutes. Add the chopped and skinned tomatoes or, if you cannot find large ripe tomatoes use a dessertspoon of tomato paste diluted with water and add the ink from the octopus to it. Add enough water to cover and cook until the octopus is quite tender. Throw in the rice and cook rapidly until all the liquid in the pan has been absorbed. Then take it out of the fire and place a dry clean cloth over the pan to keep the steam in, for ten minutes before serving.

Stewed Snails / Salingaria Yahni

2 pounds snails
3 onions
1 can tomatoes
1 tablespoon tomato paste
1/2 cup olive oil
Salt and pepper

Soak the snails in cold water overnight. Be sure to cover tightly. In the morning wash them several times, place in two quarts salted water, bring to a boil, remove immediately and drain. Chop the onions and fry them in olive oil, until soft. Add tomato paste, tomatoes, salt and pepper, cover and cook over medium flame for ten minutes. Add the snails and 3/4 cup water. Stir and cook for twenty minutes. Serve very hot with their sauce. To extract the snails from their shell use large plastic toothpicks.

Mussels With Rice / Midia Pilafi

Mussels
2 onions
1 cup rice
1 cup olive oil
1 teaspoon tomato paste
Salt.

Soak 2-3 dozen mussels in cold water for half an hour and then scrape to remove any hairy tuft or rough spots of the shell. Clean well. Brown the onions, finely chopped in hot olive oil and add the tomato paste, half a cup of water and the mussels. Cover the pan and boil until the mussels open. Remove the stubborn ones and add the rice with more water. Season, cover and cook until the rice is tender. Leave the mussels in their shell all the time.

Fish Roe Patties / Taramokeftedes

6 ounces tarama
2 potatoes
1 onion
1 dessertspoon parsley
1 dessertspoon mint
Flour.
Olive oil
Salt and pepper

Keep the tarama in boiling water for ten minutes then rinse and remove the membranes and scales. Place it in a large bowl and mix with rotary beater to thin paste. Mash the boiled potatoes thoroughly and add to tarama, blending well. Add the onion, peeled and grated and the remainder of ingredients and mix well. Form into patties, roll in flour, and fry in hot olive oil until well browned.

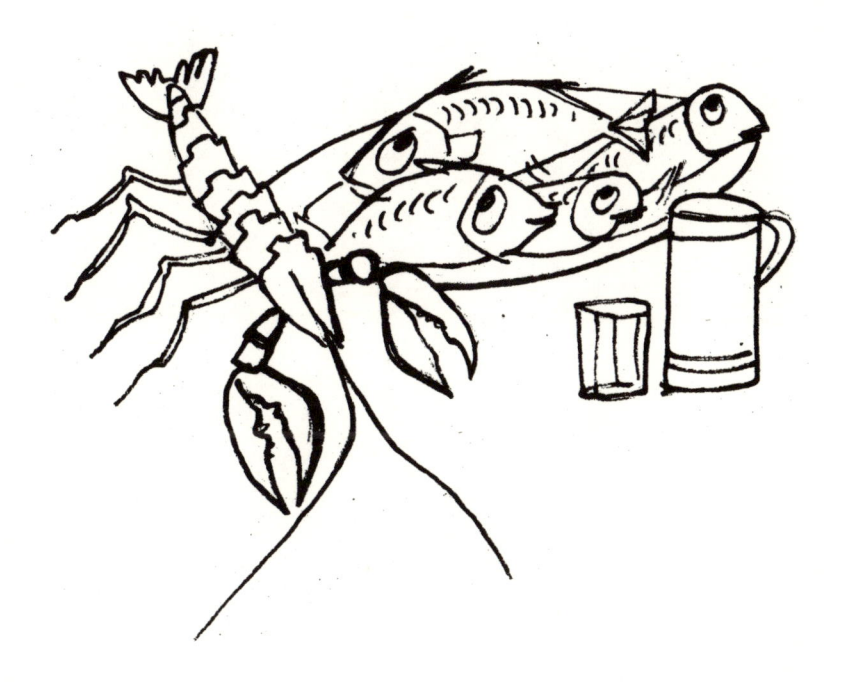

PART IV

THE TRIPTYCH

You must wake and call me early,
call me early, mother dear;
To-morrow 'll be the happiest time
of all the glad New-year;
of all the glad New-year, mother,
the maddest merriest day;
For I'm to be Queen o' the May, mother,
I'm to be Queen o' the May.

                Lord Alfred Tennyson: The May Queen

Easter-Christmas-New Year compose the *triptych* that rings in my ears like *"lovers' sonnets turn'd to holy psalms."* Because these occasions also compose the *triptych* of pastry, and cake and cookie.

I used to glue my nose to the windows of the toy-shops on Christmastime but my nose got glued with honey on Red Thursday, when the eggs were dyed and the *melomakarouna* baked. Boy oh boy how I loved mother's *kourabiedes* and especially those tiny loaves of Holy Bread with a bright red egg stuck in the dough before baking. And those crisp doughnut-shaped *koulourakia*.

I could hardly wait for the church-bells to ring the "Christ is risen" on midnight Holy Saturday and fill my heart with joy. I had a hard time keeping my eyes open to marvel the Resurrection fireworks but my stomach kept me awake just the same, thinking of *mayeritsa* and breaking my brothers' eggs to claim them as my own.

I could never get tired eating mother's *melomakarouna* and *kourabiedes*. I could eat them all the way until Christmas when the home preparations start all over again. And I could sing the *kalanda* all day for a piece of delicious *christopsomo*.

And the New Year's eve and the cutting of the *vassilopitta*. *"Burning with high hope, shall woulder cold and low"* Lord Byron sings in his *Childe Harold* and I was burning with high hope of finding the lucky gold sovereign piece hidden in the *vassilopitta*. As every piece was cut and given to my parents, the guests, and my older brothers and sisters and no coin was found my excitement was rising, and rising and rising— because I was last in line...

FOR YOUR SWEET TOOTH

"The inhabitants met them with kindness and gave them their honey-sweet flower-food to eat, but those who tasted it, only a few fortunately, lost their longing for home. They wanted only to dwell in the Lotus Land, and let the memory of all that had been fade from their minds. Odysseus had to drag them on shipboard and chain them there. They wept, so great was their desire to stay, tasting forever the honey-sweet flowers."

Odysseus in the land of Lotus Eaters

Greeks are notorious Lotus Eaters and lovers of honey-sweet flowers. When you enter a Greek house it is unthinkable to let you go without offering you something for your sweet tooth.

Greek housewives pride themselves for their own preserves made of *kidoni* (quince), *nerantzi* (bitter orange), *triantafilo* (rose petals), *melitzanaki* (baby eggplant), *kerasi* (cherry), *vissino* (sour cherry), and a thousand and one other varieties. Even if it just happens that the hostess runs out of *glyko,* spoon sweet, she will give you the opportunity to taste some delicious honey from Mount Hymetus, poured over shelled almonds and walnuts.

While Greek-American housewives try to learn how to use the *filo,* the paper thin pastry and pie sheets in preparing sweets—*baklava, kataifi* and *galaktoboureko*—in addition to their *tiropittas* and *spanakopittas,* Greek housewives specialize in preserves and rich cream cakes, especially cream *karamele.*

Cakes made of sesame and honey, sweetmeats, cheese cakes and cream cakes, and a hecatomb of new laid eggs were all devoured by us.

Atheneus tells us in his *Deipnosophists.*

Hardly a day in the Greek calendar is not a special occasion for a rich dessert. Namesdays of each member of the family alone are enough to fill-in-between holidays as an occasion to bake some kind of lucious pastry, the housewife takes pride in preparing. And, of course, she has her own way of baking *koulourakia* and all kinds of cookies, not to speak of her *melomakarouna, loukoumades, diples* and *kourabiedes* for Easter and Xmas, and *moustalevria,* wine pudding, during the vintage season.

If Athenaeus was alive today, he could easily write another *Deipnosophists* 20-volume masterpiece simply to tell us how Greeks prepare their pastries, the non-ending variety of sweets, cakes and biscuits.

In our journey through this labyrinth we tried to get Ariadne's ball of thread to retrace our steps. Fortunately we did not have to promise to take her back to Athens and marry her, since she was very happy in America. Thus, our journey in the land of Lotus Eaters was a honey-sweet one...

GET FILO

Getting *filo* in Greek means to get a lover, a sweetheart. If your hearts love sweets, get *filo*. No Greek housewife, no matter how amateur she is in the kitchen, can ignore the importance of *filo*. Because although basically used in making pastries, *filo* is equally indispensable in many meat, cheese and vegetable dishes.

Do not ever try to make *filo* yourself. It is a *Mission Impossible* without the slightest hope of success. It's easier to pass an elephant from a keyhole and besides why bother. It is always available in Greek groceries, sold by the pound and rolled thinner than the paper in this book, as it should be.

Greek housewives keep their *filo* (lover) happy and their *filo* (dough) moist. They always use one sheet at a time and have the rest covered with a damp kitchen cloth at all times. They have a way to cut it in the desired size with a razor blade and their little secret in using it properly consists of a soft brush and plenty of hot butter. There is no skimping on butter on every sheet and this makes the pastries or pies crisp and flaky. The best way to learn the use of *filo* is to try your luck in *baklava*, the king of Greek pastries and leader of the "triumvirate" of Greek sweets, with *galaktoboureko* and *kataifi*.

Baklavas

1 pound filo	1 cup honey
2 cups walnuts	8 ounces butter
2 cups sugar	1 lemon, cinnamon

In a cup of hot water add one cup of sugar and half the butter. In making *baklava* always use unsalted butter. Chop the walnuts and add them. Heat gently. Brush your baking-tin with melted butter and line four sheets of *filo* brushing each one with butter. Fill with the walnut mixture, sprinkle with cinnamon and continue by covering the filling with two more sheets of buttered *filo*. Repeat with filing and cover with two more buttered sheets of *filo*. Be careful to spread the filing evenly and tuck the sides and ends in. Use three-four sheets to cover the last layer and baste liberally with melted butter. Use a sharp knife to score the shape of pieces you desire—usualy diamonds—and bake in a moderate oven. You can increase the heat after 45 minutes until the top becomes golden brown and crisp. In the meantime prepare the syrup by bowling in one cup of water, one cup of sugar and one cup of honey. Add the juice of a lemon. Pour the syrup over the *baklava* hot and let it settle. Cut the scored pieces through to allow the *baklava* to absorb as much syrup as possible, before serving. Make sure the *baklava* is already cool before you pour the hot syrup on it. If you use almonds instead of walnuts, use the same amount. Chop and blanch them. Be careful to remove even the slightest impurity from the nuts. Always use the best quality of ingredients in making sweets and pastries.

Custard Pie / Galatoboureko

1 pound filo
2 cups milk
6 eggs
4 ounces butter
1 pound sugar
6 ounces semolina
1 teaspoon vanilla essence
1 lemon
Salt

Add to the milk six ounces of sugar, two ounces of butter with a pinch of salt, the vanilla essence, the semolina and a couple of lemon peels. Bring to the boiling point stirring constantly to make the mixture even, smooth and thick. Boil for a few minutes and then take it out of the fire and continue to stir without interruption to prevent the formation of lumps or crust. After it cools beat the eggs well, add them to the mixture and stir until even. Prepare your baking-tin as in *baklava*, but, in *galatoboureko* you should line up half of the sheets of *filo*, one on top of the other, brushing them with melted butter as you proceed. Pour the filling and spread it evenly. Cover with the remaining *filo* working in the same manner as in the bottom. Make sure in trimming the edges to fold in carefully to keep the filling well contained. Use a little cold water to seal the edges. Better use a razor blade in scoring the diamonds as in *baklava*. *Galatoboureko* is baked in the same manner until golden brown. Also prepared in the same way is the syrup. Boil it for about ten minutes until it thickens and pour it over the *galatoboureko* as it is removed from the oven using a tablespoon and distributing the syrup all around the top, little by little. *Galatoboureko* as most of the *filo* pastries should never be served hot. And they taste better the next day.

Kataifi

1 pound *kataifi*
1 pound almonds
    and walnuts
4 ounces butter

10 ounces sugar
1/2 cup honey
1 teaspoon cinnamon
1 lemon

If making *filo* is a *Mission Impossible*, making *kataifi* is next to impossible. However, if you are looking for a fascinating hobby, how about starting with this one? You may become the talk of the town and develop it into a profitable business too. All you need is a large round disc that can be heated underneath and rotate at the same time. If you can develop a range with a single giant disc, that can be heated and rotate at the same time, like a turntable, then you are in business. Next, you need a hopper that can be hanged above the rotating disc and feed a fine stream of a batter of flour and water in ever-widening circles. The heat turns the batter into a thread-like *kataifi* and all you have to do is to scoop in loops with your hand before it becomes overcooked and brittle. Now that you know how *kataifi* is made, go to a Greek grocery and buy a pound of it. And, if you cannot find it do not despair. You can prepare just as good *kataifi* pastry with shredded wheat.

Brush your baking-tin with melted butter, melt the rest of it and mix it with three ounces of sugar, the chopped nuts and cinnamon. Line half of the *kataifi* threads on the tin, spread the mixture on top of it and cover with the remaining *kataifi*. Be sure the *kataifi* threads are fresh. Mark the top into squares and bake in a moderate oven until brown. In the meantime prepare the syrup. Heat a cup of water with the remaining sugar, add the honey and the juice of a lemon and bring it to the boiling point. Then let it cool a little and pour it over the *kataifi*. Let it soak well and then cut into squares for serving. This is a standard way of making *kataifi* if served with a scoop of whipped cream or vanilla ice cream (here goes your calories schedule!). If you like to make *kataifi* in rolls stuffed individually, this is the way to proceed:

Take half a handful of *kataifi* and spread it on the palm of the left hand. Place a tablespoon of nut filling on it. Roll it like a piece of shredded wheat and press the two edges in. Place the rolls side by side in the baking-tin, greased with melted butter. Baste with melted butter and bake in a moderate oven for half an hour. Meanwhile, boil the syrup ingredients together, as above, and baste the *kataifi* with the hot syrup as soon as it comes out of the oven. Cover the baking pan with a thick napkin so that the vapor will soften the dry surface. Let it cool before serving.

Kourabiedes

      6 cups flour   *3/4 cup almonds*
      1 pound butter   *and walnuts*
      1/4 cup cream   *1/4 cup powdered sugar*
      1 egg   *Cloves*

First melt the butter over medium flame, stirring occasionally until you bring to boil. Take it away from the fire and let it stand until the butter's salt forms a scum on top. Remove the scum with a spoon and if the butter is not clear of salt, allow to boil for a couple of minutes and again skim off of the top the scum. Butter must be very clear, to succeed with *kourabiedes*.

Although you should use unsalted butter be careful not to leave any salt particles in it. Pour the butter very slowly into a mixing bowl in order to leave any particles of salt to the bottom. Add to the bowl the powdered sugar, the yolk of the egg and the cream. While mixing add flour gradually. Knead vigorously for about half an hour to make the dough crumbly but smooth. Add the nuts and continue kneading until the nuts are thoroughly mixed into dough. Be careful to have the nuts chopped fine. Take small amounts at a time from the dough and make half moon shapes, heart shapes or star shapes. Center each one with a clove bud and place about an inch apart on a cookie sheet. Bake in moderate oven until golden brown. It takes about 45 minutes. Have the powdered sugar into a bowl and when the cakes are done, roll in sugar carefully until well coated. Arrange on a platter and sift the remaining sugar over them. Make sure they are heavily coated with powdered sugar.

Greek housewives love to develop their own ways of preparing *kourabiedes*. Here they are two more, one with rose water and the other with vanilla essence:

      1 pound flour   *1/2 teaspoon baking soda*
      8 ounces butter   *1 dessertspoon brandy*
      4 ounces almonds   *1 egg*
      4 ounces sugar   *Rose water*
      4 ounces powdered sugar   *Salt*

First beat the butter with four ounces of sugar until it becomes white and creamy. Add the brandy and a well beaten egg yolk, followed by the sieved flour, baking soda, pinch of salt and ground almonds. Knead well for a few minutes and form into balls about the size of an egg. Flatten slightly as you place them to a greased baking-sheet. Bake in a cool oven for twenty minutes until the *kourabiedes* become firm and crisp but not browned. While still warm from the oven, sprinkle each one with a little rose water and dredge very liberally with the powdered sugar.

To make the vanilla flavored ones skip the almonds from the ingredients and add cloves and one tablespoon of *ouzo* and a teaspoon of vanilla essence. Mix the flour with the baking-powder and then add the butter with the sugar and then add the *ouzo* and the vanilla, the egg yolks and gradually enough flour to make a soft but firm dough. If there is not enough liquid, add either some more *ouzo* or another egg yolk. If you have made the dough too loose, then add more flour. Insert the cloves to the center of *kourabiedes* before cooking and when you take them from the oven and while still hot sprinkle with rosewater. When they are cool enough sprinkle liberally with powdered sugar.

Phoenicean Honey Cakes / Melomakarouna

4 cups farina
2 cups olive oil
2 cups honey
1 cup sugar
1/2 cup powdered sugar
1 cup walnuts

2 small glasses brandy
1 orange
1 teaspoon grated orange peel
1/2 teaspoon cinnamon
1/2 teaspoon cloves
2 teaspoons baking powder

Melomakarouna are also called *finikia,* apparently because the recipe was brought to Greece by the Phoenicians. These small honey cakes are a traditional pastry not only for the Easter, Christmas and New Year celebrations, but for practically every occasion, like Independence Day or any namesday. Every pastry shop in Greece has *melomakarouna* available at all times and Greek pastry shops in America and elsewhere have them too.

First work the farina with the olive oil until it becomes creamy. Add the powdered sugar, and a cup of lukewarm honey and the remaining ingredients, except the sugar and walnuts. Mix well. Add a little more brandy if the dough is too stiff, or add a little farina if the dough is too soft. Take a little piece of the dough at a time and roll it with your hands into the size of an egg, flattening a little on one side. Place each "egg" on a baking pan, and make a design, crosswise, with a fork. Bake in a moderate oven for about twenty minutes. Meanwhile, boil the sugar and honey and as soon as the *melomakarouna* are ready, dip each one into the hot syrup, let it stay for a couple of minutes and then take it out, drain it, place it on a platter and sprinkle with the walnuts, chopped.

Stuffed Rolls / Floyeres

6 sheets filo
10 ounces sugar
1 egg
4 ounces almonds or walnuts
1 lemon, butter
1 stick cinnamon

If you need to make more than two dozens of *floyeres* add 1 sheet of *filo* to every four *floyeres*. Make the filling first. Blanch and either grind or crush the nuts and mix them with the egg and two ounces of sugar. Cut each sheet of *filo* into four strips and brush each strip with butter. Put a teaspoonful of the filling to the end of each strip and roll up. Arrange these on a buttered baking-tin and bake in a moderate oven until golden brown. In a cup of water put half a pound of sugar, a teaspoon of lemon juice and a stick of cinnamon into a shallow pan and bring to boil. Then simmer until the syrup is of a medium thickness. As soon as the turnovers are ready, take them from the oven and placing them into a perforated spoon, dip them into the simmering syrup. Do this once or twice then put the rolls in a large platter. When all the rolls have been dipped in the syrup leave them until cold. *Floyeres* should always been served cold.

Bows / Diples

5 eggs
2-1/2 cup farina
2 oranges
1 lemon
1-1/2 cup nuts
1-1/2 cup honey
1 tablespoon cinnamon
1 teaspoon baking powder

Place in a bowl the yolk and white of the eggs and add the juice of two oranges and a lemon, and a cup of farina. Work with your hand to mix it and make a stiff dough like in bread.

If the dough is too soft, add a little more farina. Take a piece and roll it out on a floured board like a pie crust. With a pastry wheel, cut in strips about three inches long and two inches wide. Fold the two ends to form a triangle and press with the fingers to stick. Make different shapes with the strips, such as a tie, bow, triangle, or pleats. In the meantime, have a deep frying pan ready with olive oil hot enough to steam. Fry four to five pieces of the strips for 2-3 minutes until they become golden and drain while removing from the pan. Place on a dish until all the strips are fried. Then prepare the syrup. Boil the honey with half a cup of water. Arrange a layer of the *diples* in a platter, sprinkle with chopped nuts, cinnamon and the hot syrup. Arrange another layer on top and continue until all the *diples* are sprinkled with nuts and syrup. Most of the syrup will drip down in the platter, but it can be poured over the *diples* again when served in individual plates. *Diples* are usually eaten with the fingers as they break if pierced with a fork. Always serve *diples* cold.

Honey Puffs / Loukoumades

1 pound flour
4 ounces yeast
Seed oil
1 cup honey

1 teaspoon cinnamon
1 lemon
Milk and salt

Dissolve the yeast in a pan with some lukewarm milk. Add a little flour to make a dough. Let it rise in a warm place and add flour and enough lukewarm water to make a batter soft enough to be able to drop from a spoon. Cover the pan and let it stand 5-6 hours until it starts to bubble on top. Only then it is ready for frying. In a deep saucepan pour about four inches of seed oil and heat. When steaming hot, drop the batter using a spoon of it at a time and fry to a gold color. The spoon should be dipped in a cup of cold water each time you drop a spoonful of the batter. This so that the batter will not stick on spoon. When the *loucoumades* are fried drain them using absorbent paper. Arrange them on a platter and sprinkle with the syrup made with the honey and cinnamon. *Loucoumades* should always be served hot.

Halva / Halvas

8 ounces fine semolina
1 pound sugar
4 ounces almonds

4 ounces butter
4 eggs
1 teaspoon cinnamon
1 lemon

First beat the butter with 8 ounces of sugar until white and fluffy. Next beat the eggs and add them to the mixture. Add cinnamon, ground almonds and the semolina. Pour into a well-greased baking-tin and cook in a moderate oven for one hour. Make the syrup with the rest of the sugar, a cup of water and the lemon juice and boil until it begins to thicken. Remove it from the fire and cool slightly before pouring over the *halva*, when it is cooked but still warm.

Custard Pie / Bougatsa

1 pound *filo*
1 pound sugar
3 cups milk
6 eggs
6 ounces semolina
1 ounce butter
Cinnamon
Powdered sugar

Heat the milk. Beat the egg yolks until white and creamy and add the sugar and semolina. Gradually add the hot milk stirring continuously. Return the mixture to the pan and over moderate flame stir all the time until the mixture thickens. Add the butter and remove from the fire to cool. Beat the egg whites until they form peaks and fold lightly into the cooled mixture. In a well-oiled shallow baking-tin line half the *filo* brushing each sheet with melted butter and smooth them one on top of the other. Spread the filling evenly and cover with the remaining *filo*, again brushing each sheet with melted butter. Fold in the sides and ends to prevent the filling from coming out and with a razor blade, score the top two sheets into the desired size of pieces. Cover with grease-proof paper and put into a hot oven. Reduce the heat and do not remove from the oven until golden brown and crisp. This will take about thirty minutes. While still hot, sprinkle the top with powdered sugar and cinnamon. *Bougatsa* can be served either hot or *cold*.

Svigoi

1 cup flour
1/2 ounce butter
3 eggs
1 cup olive oil
1 teaspoon baking soda
Salt, honey, cinnamon

In a cup of water heat the butter. Add a teaspoon of salt. Just before boiling point is reached, add the flour and baking soda and stir vigorously until the paste leaves the sides of the pan.

Draw away from the fire and rest for a few minutes. Break the eggs one by one and work into the mixture. Beat vigorously for fifteen minutes until the mixture is even. Leave for three hours before cooking. The more you work the eggs in the mixture the better *svigoi* will get. In a deep pan heat the olive oil and when very hot, take a teaspoonful of the mixture and drop it into the pan. One at a time. When the *svigoi* surface, turn them over and cook until golden. Remember, the *svigoi* should be very light and fluffy and should be served hot with warmed honey and cinnamon or a syrup of sugar and water.

Fritters / Tiganites

6 teaspoon flour
1/2 teaspoon baking soda
Olive oil
Salt, sugar, cinnamon and honey

This is a "poor man's dessert" Greek housewives prepare in a jiffy to satisfy a sudden urge for sweet dessert in the family.

Sieve the flour before mixing in a cup of water. Add the baking soda and salt. Mix to a stiff dropping consistency. With a wooden spoon, beat the batter well until smooth and creamy and leave to stand for half an hour. Heat well a cup of olive oil in a frying-pan and drop in one dessertspoonful of the batter at a time. Fry quickly on both sides until golden. Place the *tiganites* on a large dish and pour over them some warmed honey, sprinkle with cinnamon and sugar and serve at once.

Wheat Pudding / Poutingha

1 quart milk
3/4 cup cream of wheat
1/3 cup pecans
1/2 cup butter
1 cup sugar
1 teaspoon vanilla
1 teaspoon cinnamon

Boil the milk adding the butter and sugar. Add gradually the cream of wheat stirring all the time. When it begins to bubble take it out of the fire and let it cool stirring from time to time to prevent crusting. Beat the eggs and add them to the mixture. Then pour it into a baking tin after you brush it well with melted butter. Bake in a moderate oven for about half an hour, remove and top with the usual sugar syrup. Let it cool for about three hours before serving. You can garnish *poutingha* with chopped nuts or fruit salad.

Scaltsounia

1 pound flour	1 teaspoon baking powder
1 cup olive oil	1 lemon
1 pound almonds and walnuts	1 teaspoon m a s t i h a crystals
1 teaspoon cloves	Powdered sugar
1 teaspoon cinnamon	Honey

First blanch and crush the nuts. Mix them with ground cinnamon, ground cloves and the powdered m a s t i h a crystals you can find in all Greek groceries. Add enough honey to blend the mixture without making it too stiff. Next mix in a cup of water the baking powder and the olive oil. Add the juice of the lemon and add enough flour to make a stiff dough. Roll the dough on a board sprinkled with flour. Be careful to roll the dough to a thickness of about one third of an inch. Cut the dough in circles using a cup. Put on each circle a teaspoonful of the nut filling and fold over the filling. Press the edges of the dough together. Arrange on a greased baking pan and bake for about 15 minutes in a moderate oven until the *scaltsounia* become golden brown. Leave until cool enough to handle, then dip them into rose water and sprinkle with powdered sugar generously.

Almond Crispies / Amygdalota

2 pounds almonds	4 eggs
1-1/2 cups sugar	2 teaspoons rose water

Mix the sugar and the almonds finely chopped. Beat the egg whites until stiff and fold in the almonds and sugar. Blend together and add rose water. With a teaspoon take a piece of the mixture and place it on a greased cookie sheet. Bake in a moderate oven for fifteen minutes. This posology should be enough for 2-1/2 dozen of *amygdalota*.

BAKE A CAKE

Greeks bake a cake—as their pastries—mostly for special occasions. They bake a *Lambropsomo* for Easter, *Christopsomo* for Christmas and *Vassilopitta* for New Year, and they bake *tsourekia* all year around. They bake their *pantespani* and when the vintage season comes they get some *mousto*, wine yeast to make their most delicious *moustokouloura* and their *moustalevria*—the kind of custard I was waiting all year to have my mother make for me.

Most of the Greek bakery shops here in America and all the pastry shops in Greece make good business with these special occasion cakes and if you happen to like them you can buy them ready made practically at any time. But you cannot be sure they will taste the same as the ones made by a knowledgeable Greek housewife. How she does it? Just follow the instructions and never skimp on the ingredients.

New Year Cake / Vassilopitta

6 eggs	2 ounces yeast
3 pounds flour	1 teaspoon cinnamon
1 cup milk	1/2 teaspoon
3 ounces sugar	sesame seeds
4 ounces butter	Salt

Use a large mixing bowl to work. First crumble the yeast into it. Warm up the milk and add half of it. Add half a teaspoon of salt and enough flour—four to five teaspoons—to make a batter. Work with your hands. Cover with a napkin and let it settle in a warm place. It will rise. Until then—it takes about an hour—put the remaining flour in another large mixing bowl. Make a well in the centre, stir in the yeast batter. Melt the butter and add it with the eggs, one at a time, sesame, and the remaining milk. Mix thoroughly. Knead for at least ten minutes until the dough is stiff; if it is not, add more flour; if too stiff, add more milk. Cover the dough again and leave to rise, this time for three hours. Spread the dough on a floured board and knead as you would for making a loaf of bread. Tear off a handful and shape the remainder into a cake. Place it into a greased baking tin but leave space for further rising. Take most of the torn-off piece of dough and form it into a long sausage shape with your hands and arrange in a circle on top of the cake. Inside this circle some like to design the numbers of the coming year with the remaining dough. Cover the dough again with a napkin and let it rise another inch. Push a coin into the cake, beat the remaining egg with a little warm water and sugar and brush this over the top before putting it into the oven. Bake in a moderate oven until brown. You can sprinkle chopped almonds over the top of the *Vassilopitta* before baking, if you like.

Easter Bread / Lambropsomo

2 pounds flour
1 egg
5 red eggs
1/4 cup milk
2 ounces yeast
1 orange
Olive oil
Sesame seeds, salt

Warm the milk and dissolve the yeast in it. Let it stand for ten minutes then add gradually four ounces of flour. Mix it and cover with a napkin. Leave it in a warm place overnight to rise. In the morning put the remaining flour in a large bowl and make a well in the centre. Add salt and half a cup of lukewarm water and gradually work the yeast batter into the centre of the well, adding as you go the other half cup of lukewarm water. When all the flour is mixed into the batter, knead the dough for at least ten minutes. Add a peel from the orange. If the dough is too loose add a little more flour. Brush a board with olive oil and sprinkle it generously with sesame seeds. Take enough of the dough from it and shape into a long loaf, then roll it over and over in the sesame seeds. Pat the loaf until it is about two inches high. Take the remaining dough and divide it into two pieces. Roll them with the hands into long sausage-shape rolls about twice the length of the loaf. Cover with sesame seeds and when well covered place it along one side of the loaf, pressing it down slightly. Do the same with the other piece but place this on the other side of the loaf. Make five depressions in the loaf, one in the centre, the others at the four points to form a cross. Put into them the red eggs. Leave covered with a napkin for about three hours. Beat the egg yolk with a tablespoon of cold water and lightly brush the top of the loaf. Bake in a hot oven for about 45 minutes, until the bread is a golden brown.

To make *Christopsomo*, or Christmas bread, use the same recipe and procedure. But instead of red eggs make a cross and garnish with chopped nuts.

Easter Cake / Tsoureki

For the ingredients and the preparation of the dough proceed in the same manner as for making a *Vassilopitta*. Make the dough a little more stiff to avoid its spreading while baking. To mold each *tsoureki* take three lumps of dough, the size of an orange. With the palms of your hands roll each lump on a floured board to no more than ten inches in length. The rolled dough should be thicker in the middle and pointed at the ends.

Roll each of the last pieces into a long rope. Braid three of the "ropes" into a twisted loaf and place on a buttered baking sheet. Cover the loaves and let them rise in a warm place, until they are doubled in bulk. Brush with the beaten egg. Bake in a preheated moderate oven for half an hour. If you like you can make depressions on the loafs before baking and place red eggs. This only if you make *tsourekia* for Easter, of course. There are *tsourekia* available in Greek pastry shops all year around.

Bagels / Koulourakia

4 cups flour
1/2 cup sugar
2 eggs
1/3 cup milk
1/3 cup butter
1 teaspoon vanilla essence

First cream the sugar, butter and vanilla essence thoroughly. Add an egg yolk and white and beat well, then add the other and continue beating thoroughly. Next add the milk and flour alternately, beating vigorously to blend well. Work with your hands until a smooth dough is obtained. Sprinkle flour on a board and roll the mixture. Take a small portion at each time, and roll out into donut shape with your hands. Sesame seeds may be sprinkled on the board and rolled into the dough, if you like. Brush the top of the *koulourakia* with beaten egg and bake in greased cookie sheet for twenty minutes in moderate oven.

Wine Must Bagels / Moustokouloura

2 cup wine must, drained
3 tablespoons honey
1 teaspoon cinnamon
1 tablespoon baking soda, flour

First boil the wine must. When reduced to half its volume, add the honey. Let it cool and then add cinnamon and baking soda. Place in a bowl and mix in enough flour to make a stiff dough as for cookies. Set aside for half an hour. Take a small piece of dough, place on a floured board and shape in small round rolls or in any cooky shape desired. Continue until all the dough is shaped. Bake in a moderate oven for about twenty minutes.

Angel Food Cake / Pantespani

4 cups flour
12 eggs
2 cups sugar
Olive oil, sugar syrup

Beat the sugar with the eggs thoroughly until light and fluffy. Sift the flour and fold slowly into the mixture. Grease a tube pan with olive oil and pour the mixture slowly. Bake in moderate oven for one hour. Top with the usual sugar syrup.

Copenhagen/Kopenhaghi

1 pound of almonds
1-1/2 pounds powdered sugar
1 cup butter
4 cups flour
12 eggs
1 tablespoon cognac
1 tablespoon nutmeg
1 tablespoon cinnamon
6 biscuits
1 tablespoon baking powder

This very popular Greek pastry is simply another variation of the almond cake and no one knows why it is named after the capital of Danemark. Apparently to honor the ex-royal house of Greece that originated from Danemark. Chop the almonds finely. Melt the butter and add the egg yolks beating vigorously. Add half of the sugar and blend well. Gradually add flour and baking powder and mix until a smooth dough is obtained. Mould for about five minutes. Roll out into a baking pan allowing for the dough to be pressed firmly to the bottom of the pan and extending over the edges for about half an inch. Mix the chopped almonds, biscuit crumbs, cinnamon and nutmeg in a large bowl. In another bowl put the remaining sugar. Beat the egg whites until stiff and gently fold into the nut mixture, blending well. Pour this mixture into the pan with the original mixture and press firmly to even.

Bake for ten minutes in a preheated in moderate heat oven and then reduce the heat gradually, until the *kopenhaghi* becomes golden brown. When the *kopenhaghi* is done, remove the paper and pour the usual sugar syrup slowly over, so it will absorb easily. Let it settle for six hours before cutting. Cut into diamond shapes to serve.

Ravani

1 pound flour
1 pound sugar
7 eggs
3/4 pound butter
1 lemon
Sugar syrup

Blend the melted butter with the sugar thoroughly with a mixer. Add the egg yolks, the juice of one lemon and the flour and mix well. Whip the whites from the eggs until stiff and combine with mixture. Pour into a buttered pan and bake in moderate oven half an hour. That's all. *Ravani* you can topple with ice cream. If not, then topple with the usual pastry syrup, not too thick. You can also flavor with vanilla essence as in *kourabiedes* and add a teaspoon of baking soda to make more fluffy. Half a cup of chopped blanched almonds can also be added for another variation.

Nut Cake / Savaren

6 tablespoon of sugar
6 eggs
6 tablespoons of biscuit crumbs
1/3 cup peas
1/2 teaspoon cloves
1/2 teaspoon cinnamon
Sugar syrup

Another variation of the nut category of cakes is the *savaren*—very popular in Greek pastry shops. Mix the cinnamon, cloves and biscuit crumbs. Beat the eggs well and add the sugar continuing beating until all is well blended. Work with your hands adding the biscuit mixture and then the pecans chopped finely. After they are thoroughly mixed, pour into a well greased pan and bake for half an hour in moderate oven. Watch carefully not to scorch. While still hot top with sugar syrup prepared in the usual manner. Let stand six hours before cutting and serving.

Nut Rolls / Saraili

1 pound *filo*
2 cups almonds and walnuts
1/2 cup powdered sugar
1 cup butter
1 tablespoon cinnamon
Syrup

Chop the nuts finely. Place a sheet of *filo* on a table and sprinkle it with nuts. Lay another sheet on top and sprinkle with nuts. Continue in this manner until you make eight "floors." Cover with a ninth sheet and roll tightly lengthwise to make a "sausage." Be sure you keep your *filo* moist at all times as directed previously. Slice the rolls to pieces of about an inch and a half each and place in a baking tin. Arrange them tightly. Melt the butter and pour a tablespoon of it over each roll. Bake in moderate oven for about 45 minutes or until they get golden brown. Pour over the rolls sugar syrup made the usual way. Let it stand on the tin for a couple of hours and then place them on a large platter and sprinkle generously with the powdered sugar mixed with a tablespoon of cinnamon.

Walnut Pie/Karydopitta

3 cups flour
1/2 cup butter
1-1/2 cups sugar
4 cups walnuts
3 teaspoons baking powder
1 teaspoon cinnamon
6 eggs
Salt

Mix the flour with the chopped walnuts. Add the cinnamon, baking powder and half teaspoon of salt. Mix well the butter and sugar and break in the eggs, one at a time, stirring well. Mix with the other ingredients to form a smooth paste and spread on a greased baking pan. Bake in a moderate oven for half an hour.

As soon as the *karydopitta* comes out of the oven, pour over the usual sugar syrup. Let cool and then cut in squares.

Almond Cake/Migdalopitta

1 pound filo
1-1/2 pounds almonds
12 eggs
2 cups biscuit crumbs
6 ounces butter
3 cups sugar, sugar syrup

First blanch the almonds and chop them finely. Mix them with the biscuit crumbs. Beat the eggs and as you beat them continuously add the sugar and the almond mixture. Mix thoroughly. Melt the butter over low flame. Brush a baking pan generously with butter. Arrange half of the *filo* at the bottom of the pan, brushing every other one with butter. Pour in the filling and place the remainder of *filo* on top, also brushing every other one with butter. Bake in moderate oven for about an hour. While it is still warm pour over it a usual sugar syrup prepared with a slice of lemon added. Leave the *migdalopitta* stand overnight before cutting the cake to pieces and serving like *ravani*.

Honey Pie / Melopitta

1 pound flour	6 ounces sugar
8 ounces honey	6 ounces butter
6 eggs, salt	1-1/2 teaspoons baking powder
1-1/2 pounds cottage cheese	2 teaspoons cinnamon

With your hands work the flour with water. Add the baking-powder, a little salt and the butter. Add enough water to make a stiff dough. Roll out and line a pie tin. Next, mix the cheese, sugar and half the cinnamon in a bowl. Add the honey and when this is thoroughly blended, add the eggs, one by one, beating well. Pass the mixture through a sieve and pour it into a pie shell. Bake in a slow oven for 45 minutes, then increase the heat and bake for a further 15 minutes. When it is ready insert a knife into the filling. If it comes out clean, the pie is ready. Remove and sprinkle with the remaining cinnamon after it cools.

Yoghourt Pie / Yaourtopitta

1 cup yoghourt	6 eggs
3 cups flour	1 lemon
3 cups sugar	1 tablespoon baking soda
4 ounces butter	Salt, powdered sugar

Beat well the eggs' yolks with the yoghourt and, working with your hands, mix the butter and sugar. Add the beaten egg yolks and yoghourt. Sieve the flour with the baking soda and a pinch of salt and add slowly to the mixture with the juice and grated rind of the lemon. Beat the egg whites until they form peaks and fold into the mixture with a knife. Pour into a greased and floured cake ring and bake in a moderate oven for one hour. Turn out on to a cake rack to cool and dust with powdered sugar.

Rice Pudding / Rizogalo

1-1/2 pints milk	1 lemon
2 tablespoons sugar	1 egg,
1-1/2 tablespoons rice	Cinnamon, salt

Greeks like to make their own *rizogalo* and, of course, they have a special way of preparing it. They boil the milk, sugar and rice together with a piece of lemon peel, preferably in a double saucepan. Add a pinch of salt and cook very slowly until the rice has absorbed all the milk. Remove from the fire and cool a little before mixing in the egg yolk beaten up in a little cold milk. Cook for a few minutes longer and pour on to individual plates. When cold, sprinkle generously with cinnamon. That's all.

Cream Karamele / Krema Karamele

5 eggs	1 cup sugar
3 cups milk	Vanilla, salt

Beat the eggs lightly. Boil the milk with half the sugar and add the eggs. Stir continuously. Add a spring of vanilla and salt. Boil the other half sugar with two teaspoons of water until the syrup takes a brownish color. Have personalized baking forms. Distribute the syrup in them making sure it goes all around. Let it cool and then pour the cream in. Bake in moderate oven for half an hour. Put the forms in the frigidaire and take the *krema karamele* out only when serving.

Wine Must Custard / Moustalevria

Juice of grapes	1 cup farina
4 tablespoons honey	Walnuts or
1 teaspoon soda	sesame seeds

This is a special kind of dessert made only during the vintage season when wine must is available. You can make your own, of course, by squeezing 10 to 12 pounds of grapes. Boil the grapes' juice for an hour with three cups of water, and add the honey and the soda. Take it out of the fire and keep it covered overnight to settle. Next morning strain it through a muslin or a paper thin piece of cloth and boil it again. Then add gradually the farina stirring constantly with a wooden spoon. When it starts bubbling take it out of the fire and pour into dessert dishes. Let it cool and sprinkle it with sesame seeds or chopped walnuts.

WISH ME HRONIA POLLA

Birthdays and wedding aniversaries are usually reserved for close family celebrations in Greece but namesdays are open house affairs—unless the celebrant puts a classified ad in the newspapers informing his friends and acquaintances that, for one reason or another, or for no reason at all, he would not hold an open house on his namesday. Yet, no family will close the doors of their home in a day that one of the members celebrates his or hers namesday. The hostess is busy all day and especially all evening bringing to the living room trays full of the traditional *kafe,* coffee, and the *glyko,* a spoon sweet to give the visitors to wish the *hronia polla,* many happy returns.

A Greek house may run out of bread for a minute, but it never runs out of *glyko,* a spoon sweet. Any visitor that crosses the door of the house, anytime, is entitled to a spoon sweet. Greek housewives love to cook them as a rule, but they never eat their own *glyko.* They prefer to eat the neighbour's one and get the recipe if it happens that they like it much. *Kydoni,* quince, is the most popular and there are many different ways to prepare it, as with the other fruits.

Spoon sweets by famous pastry shops from the various areas of Greece are available in jars and imported here from Greece by Greek pastry shops in large American cities. Yet, it is fun to try and make your own if you like cooking. Only be careful when boiling the fruits, because they have a tendency to puff up and you may get burn. To avoid it use a very large saucepan and sprinkle with a teaspoon of water from time to time to prevent the fruits to puff up. And stir constantly to keep the *glyko* to an even consistency.

Grated Quince / Kydoni Kofto

2 pounds quinces
2 pounds sugar
1-1/2 cups water
1 teaspoon vanilla

First peel the quinces and grade them coarsely to the core. Put the quinces in a large saucepan with a cup of water. When it starts boiling, cover the saucepan and simmer until tender. Add the sugar gradually and boil uncovered over a high flame until syrup becomes thick. Make a test by dipping a teaspoon in the *kydoni*. Let the syrup drip down. If the last drop sticks to the tip of the spoon like a pearl, the *kydoni* is ready. Remove the saucepan from the fire and add vanilla flavoring. Let it cool a little and then pour it into jars. Leave the jars uncovered until the *kydoni* is cold.

Quince Paste / Kydonopasto

4 pounds quinces
3 pounds sugar
1 cup almonds
1 teaspoon brandy, cinnamon

This is another popular way of making a spoon sweet from *kydoni*. Prepare the quinces as in the *kydoni* recipe. Boil until tender and then press the quince through a sieve to make a pulp. Heat the sugar with a glass of the juice in a large saucepan. When it starts boiling add a glass of the pulp, mixing constantly with a wooden spoon. Continue adding a glass of the juice and a glass of the pulp at a time, mixing constantly. As soon as the mixture thickens, put your kitchen gloves on to protect your hands from the splashing and to avoid burns. Continue boiling until the mixture starts to detach itself from the bottom of the pan and is as thick as dough. Add about half a cup of blanched almonds a few minutes before removal of the *kydoni* pulp from the heat. Have a buttered shallow pan ready, and pour in the pulp. Spread evenly and set aside in a warm place, or in the sun to dry. It takes eight to ten days. Then warm the bottom of the pan and invert it on to a piece of wax paper. Let the *kydonopasto* stand for a few more days to dry completely. Brush surface with a little brandy or rum. Dust with granulated sugar and powdered cinnamon. Cut in square pieces or diamond shapes. Serve on candy dishes, or keep in candy boxes with waxed paper in between the layers.

Quince Puree / Kydoni Pelte

When you make the *kydonopasto* reserve the water after boiling the quinces. Add sugar and bring to boil. Stir continuously until the stock gets to a jellying point. Add the juice of a lemon and take out of the fire. Cool. You can make *pelte* only instead of *kydonopasto*. In such case figure the posology is 3 pounds of quince, 4 pounds of sugar and 12 cups of water. You can add blanched almonds and a teaspoon of cognac. And the juice of a lemon. The procedure is the same as in *kydonopasto* but *pelte* does not require the drying part of it.

Sour Cherry / Vissino

| 1 pound sour cherries | 1-1/2 pounds sugar 1 lemon |

Remove the pips from the *vissino* carefully and place in a large saucepan sprinkling each layer with sugar. Add half a cup of water. Cook rapidly and stir gently. Skim off any scum from the top and when the *vissino* starts to thicken add the juice from the lemon. Make the same test as in *kydoni* and if the last drop of the syrup sticks to the spoon, cook for five more minutes. The syrup should be as thick as honey by then.

Bitter Orange / Nerantzaki

To make *nerantzaki* spoon sweet first you have to find young bitter oranges, the size of a ping-pong ball. You need a gadget to remove the seeds. For every ten *nerantzakia* use a cup of sugar. Soak the *nerantzaki* in cold water overnight. In the morning, drain and put in fresh water to boil. Add half a teaspoon of soda. Boil until soft. Test with a long needle. If the *nerantzaki* slips off the needle, it is cooked. Then, drain and place in cold water for a few hours, drain again and place on a napkin to dry. Prepare the usual sugar syrup. If you have 30 *nerantzakia* use three cups of sugar and one cup of water. After you boil the syrup put the *nerantzakia* in. Simmer for ten minutes, take out of the fire and let stand in the syrup until the following day.
Keep the saucepan covered. Next morning take the *nerantzakia* out of the syrup and boil it again until it becomes thick. Then place the *nerantzakia* back in the syrup and simmer until the syrup coats them very thickly.

Bitter Orange Rolled / Nerantzi Gyristo

When bitter oranges ripe they are very large and cannot be served as a spoon sweet. Greek housewives developed a different way of preparing them as *glyko*, because, otherwise bitter oranges go to waste. First they grate them lightly, they wash them thoroughly, they cut them in four and they peel them good. Then, they fold the pieces and, with a needle and a thread, they make *komboloia*, rosaries of about fifteen pieces each, depending on the size. They tie the two ends to make a ring, the *komboloi*, and they put these rolls in a large saucepan with water. If you are doing it then be careful to cook them very soft. Let them cool, drain and put in cold water the *nerantzi* pieces—tied together—for 24 hours. Change the water from time to time. Next day take the rings out, remove the threads and let the *nerantzia* dry. In the meantime prepare the sugar syrup as indicated in the previous recipe and boil the *nerantzia* rolls in it twice until the syrup becomes honey thick.

Baby Eggplant / Melitzanaki

To make this delicious spoon sweet you need a special type of baby eggplant, ripe. With a sharp knife cut a slit and put them to boil with enough water to cover. Do not overcook because the *melitzanakia* may become a mush. Drain them and dry in a napkin and then insert a blanched almond deep inside each *melitzanaki*. Next prepare your syrup.

Figure three cups of sugar to one of water. Add some cloves to taste, a small stick of cinnamon, and pour a tablespoon of lemon juice to keep the syrup from crystallizing. When the syrup is almost done throw in the *melitzanakia* and bring to boil. Take the pan from the fire, leave to cool, then take out the *melitzanakia* carefully. Boil the syrup again, let it become thick, return the *melitzanakia*, then bring the syrup again to the boil. Handle the same way as *nerantzakia*.

Rose Petals / Triantafilo

The problem, of course, is how to find about a pound of rose petals of the special sweet-smelling type roses. There are plenty in Greece and therefore the best you can do to have some *triantafilo* spoon sweet in your house is to buy it from a Greek grocery, imported from Greece. If this sounds like the egg of Columbus, it is. Just in case you get hold of the rose petals take out the white tip from each rose petal and carefully wash them. Place a layer of sugar to the bottom of a large saucepan, add a layer of rose petals, a layer of sugar, and so forth until all the rose petals have been used. You need two pounds of sugar for one pound of rose petals. Mix the juice of a lemon in a cup of water and pour over the mixture. Bring to a boil, cover, and simmer until the mixture thickens. Some Greek housewives who make *triantafilo* from the rose petals of their own rose bushes, after cutting off the hard white base of the petal, they mix the *triantafila* with a little sugar working gently with their fingers and they cover the mixture with a napkin overnight to get the bitterness out as much as possible.

Mastic / Mastiha

The island of Chios is famous for its *mastiha*. Up in the hills the mastic shrubs are grown by the millions and they envelope the entire island with a delightful aroma when the wind comes to the town from the west. The mastic is a small crystal the same as resin used in the preparation of *retsina* wine. It is produced in the same way as resin by making incisions in the body of the shrub and make it cry. The tears fall in a layer of fine sand around the bush, gathered and cleaned by hand. *Mastiha* makes a delicious liqueur but it is also used to make a spoon sweet. First you pound enough for a teaspoon of powdered. In half a cup of water dissolve three cups of sugar and boil, add the juice of a lemon and cook for one more minute and then pour in a bowl. When this syrup is still lukewarm add the *mastiha* powder and stir with a wooden spoon until the mixture thickens and takes a milky color. If mastic crystal cannot be found in your Greek grocery store, you can substitute with a teaspoon of vanilla essence and you make another popular spoon sweet of the Greeks, the *vanilla*. Greeks like to dip a dessertspoon of these sweets in iced water, before eating slowly.

Compotes / Kombostes

Greeks like to eat their fruits either fresh or as *kombostes,* boiled with a usual sugar syrup, very light. *Kombostes* you can find in the menus of every restaurant in Greece and their mixed one are somehow not exactly like a fruit salad—which they call *froutosalata.* Their way to prepare *kombostes* is a very simple one. Here are two illustrations:

Apple Compote / Kombosta Milo

6 apples   1 lemon
1 cup sugar   Cinnamon

Peel, core and cut the apples in halves or quarters. Place them in a saucepan with a cup of water, the sugar, the juice of the lemon and a few sticks of cinnamon. Cover and cook for about half an hour. The same way you can proceed for peaches or pears. For quince it is somehow different.

Quince Compote / Kombosta Kydoni

4 quinces   3 cups sugar, cinnamon cloves

Wash and scrub the quinces but do not peel. Cut in quarters or less. Core and boil in three cups of water. Add cinnamon or cloves, or both. Cover and simmer until tender. Add the sugar and bring to a boil for another fifteen minutes. By then the *kydoni* turn to a red color. Chill before serving.

Cherry Syrup / Vissinada

There are a lot of hot days in Greece and probably the most welcome refreshment is a home made *vissinada*, prepared with the syrup of sour cherries. A couple of tablespoons of cherry syrup mixed in a glass of iced water makes, pronto, a *vissinada*. To make the syrup use two pounds of sour cherries and 2-1/2 pounds of sugar.

Wash the sour cherries and remove the stems. Pit the cherries, being careful not to crush them. Place them in layers in a wide saucepan, spreading each layer with sugar. Rinse the pits in a bowl with a couple of cups of water, and pour the liquid into the saucepan. Put on to boil until the syrup becomes thick, as explained in previous recipes. Stir gently with a large spoon, being careful not to crush the cherries. Skim the foam with a spoon strainer, dipping the spoon each time in cold water. When the syrup thickens, add the juice of a lemon. Stir a few minutes before serving. To test the syrup, place a few drops on a saucer. If the drops stay whole and do not spread, the syrup is ready. Pour in bottles and keep them open until the syrup cools completely. Then close.

Loukoumaki
(Not to be confused with LOUKOUMADES)

Loukoumaki has no relation whatsoever to *loukoumades*. Usually called turkish delight the *loukoumaki* is a gelatin like sweet prepared in many different flavors with almonds or without. While the island of Chios is famous for its *mastiha*, the island of Syros is famous for its *syriana*. The Greek equivalent of the American expression "how sweet it is!" is *loukoumaki*. When you see a sweet girl she is a *loukoumaki*. When your suit at the taylor fits perfectly it comes like a *loukoumaki*. And when in your business you make a good deal it's a *loukoumaki*. And here is how to make *loukoumaki*:

3 tablespoons jelly	Pistachio nuts
2 cups sugar	Almonds
1 orange	Powdered sugar

Dilute the jelly in half a cup of cold water and the sugar in half a cup of hot water. Put the sugar to boil and add the diluted jelly and simmer for half an hour. Peel the orange and add the juice and some rind to the mixture. Blend with a wooden spoon and strain into a flat pan large enough to allow a thickness of about an inch for the mixture. Blend the nuts in and place in the frigidaire to chill, like a usual jelly. Let it become firm and turn the mixture into a board. With a sharp knife cut it into cubes and roll them in powdered sugar. Sprinkle with more sugar the plate you pile them into.

PART V : EPILOGUE

And I will serve you up a meal
Which shall be redolent
Of the Athenian breezes

Athenaeus

INNER SANCTUM

Pardon for intruding into your *inner sanctum*, but it is for a good reason. I would like you to take a peek at a Greek housewife's own *inner sanctum* and compare. Maybe you are missing something and you like to add it to your kitchen's armory. Or may be, as an amateur, you have the curiosity to know what a Greek housewife's tools consist of. Or, since you have cookery as a hobby you like to buy some of Greece's obsolete—granted—cooking implements and hang them in the walls of your kitchen—if you find a spot—for decorative purposes. A well equipped Greek kitchen has:

- 3 sizes of baking tins called *tapsi*
- 3 sizes of aluminum frying pans called *saganaki*
- 3 sizes of pots or sauce-pans called *hytra*
- 1 large baking tin to make *mousaka, pasticcio* or bake half a lamb.
- 3 sizes of stewpans or saucepans called *katsarola*
- 2 sizes of frying pans called *tighani*
- 2 sizes of graters called *triftis*
- 2 sizes of strainers called *sourotiri*

And then they have all the usual well-known kitchen utensils including an indispensable mortar and its pestle made of special wood to stand hard pounding while making the popular *skordalia*. They also have a variety of wooden spoons and forks and board to cut the meat or knead the dough. And a copper-pan called *davas* to make *giuvetsi*. They also have a set of fancy forms to bake their cakes and a heavy wooden roller called *plastis* to spread the dough to a thick sheet. A Greek housewife who is below average in cooking experience usually gets confused in comparing the weight of different ingredients when the measurements call for a tea cup of let's say water versus sugar. Here are the comparisons in grams:

A tea cup of:	Weighs:
Fine flour	120
Chopped walnuts	125
Black raisin	125
Chopped almonds	150
Yellow raisin	150
Tiny *hilopites*	150
Powdered sugar	160
Farina	175
Navy beans	175
Rice	200
Lentils, milk, butter, sugar, olive oil, water	225
Honey	350

More important than the weight of the ingredients is, of course, the weight of the housewife and the other members of the family if they have to watch their calories. A Greek housewife knows that she should not go over 2,500 calories per day and she has a table in her *Odigos Maghirikis,* the cooking guide, to guide her on the calory value of each ingredient. And here is the table, based on 100 grams of each item:

Butter	900	Peas, lentils	330
Chopped walnuts	720	Navy beans	320
Alcohol	700	Sausages	290
Cocoa	550	Orange	280
Salami	450	Apples	250
Kasseri cheese	430	Peaches	245
Parmesan, Sugar, Ham	400	Bread, *Feta* cheese	240
Chestnuts	390	Strawberies	235
Dry cheeses	380	Pears, cherries	230
Spaghetti	350	Meat	200

Eggs are valued at 70 calories each and potatoes at 80 calories per 100 grams.
In deciding your daily menus on the basis of the schedule that follows, be very careful. Greek cookery includes a lot of sauces and pasta. It is up to you to keep a balanced daily menu and enjoy Greek cooking every day.

"EIS YGEIAN"

Go thy way, eat thy bread with joy,
and drink thy wine with a merry heart;
for God now accepteth the works
     Bible: Ecclesiastes ix 7

Eis Ygeian means "to your health" and, if you are a lover of Greek cookery, you better learn these two magic words in making a toast. Your Greek friends will be delighted and you will be on your way to an unforgettable *glendi*, a merrimaking of your life.

When Greeks speak of *glendi* they primarily mean wine. There are more Greek songs about wine than about the beautiful eyes of the maids of Athena. And Greeks would all die in two weeks if by some act of God wheat, olive oil and wine was taken away from their diet. Unbelievable as it may seem three of the twelve Greek gods at the Olympus were:

Athena, daughter of Zeus, who brought the olive tree to Athens

Dimitra, goddess of the earth, who brought wheat to Eleusis, and

Dionysus, the merriest of gods, wearing bunches of grapes as earrings.

The ancient Greek tradition was even preserved by the Orthodox faith when bread became the body of Christ and wine His blood. Bread and wine therefore are, like water, a must in the daily diet of every Greek.

Late August, when the vintage season gets into full swing, a Wine Festival is organized in the Daphni forrest preserve just a few miles from Athens and every wine producer in the country brings his specialties for tasting. This is not a usual wine tasting exhibition. This is an occasion to have an all day all night picnic with all kinds of entertainment and food and lots and lots of wines to drink to your heart's desire and your stomach's endurance.

However, a knowledgeable Greek wine drinker wants no part of a Wine Festival. He detests those tourist attractions as he detests bottled wine. He would rather walk three days and find a *taverna* offering a reputable quality of *retsina* direct from those large wooden barrels scraped good before receiving the new vintage. And he would mark it: *est, est, est* for his friends to know where to settle after the toil of the day.

Of course, to indulge in this type of wine drinking, one has to go to Greece. For the rest of us a bottle of imported Greek wine is all we can hope for. It is not too bad provided you know your wines. Here are some tips about them:

Greeks serve either *ouzo* or beer or even vermouth with their appetizers. They also serve *retsina* wines, but never a sweet wine or a heavy one called *moshato*, *mavrodafni* or champagne. These three types are served with fruits or desserts. Greeks serve *ouzo* chilled with a variety of *meze*. Ginger-ale or soda does not go with *ouzo*. Only water and ice cubes.

Red wines, of *rose* or *kokkineli* type, are served with meat, poultry and dishes that have cheese as a basic ingredient. Red wines are not served with fish. *Retsina* and white non-resin wines go well with fish.

There is quite a variety of wines in the market and if you plan to have a good selection of them in your cellar just keep in mind that white wines are served before the red ones and the dry wines before the sweet ones. And, of course, liquors are never served with a *meze*—even if the guest is not staying for dinner.

THE DAILY HEADACHE

Greek housewives have cured the headache of "what are we going to eat today?" by developing all kinds of menus based on the seasons and the calendar. Greeks eat home what the *tsoukali*—the saucepan of the mother or the wife produces. They appreciate good home cooking and a variety of it. To solve the problem Greek housewives established spring, summer, fall and winter menus as well as special ones for the lenten season, Easter, Christmas and New Year, buffet serving and, even, one to celebrate the engagement of their daughter. Let's start with this latter one:

Menu A : Variety of *meze,* cube steak with spinach souffle, potatoes. A special cake and fruits. *Ouzo* and *Rose* wine.

Menu B : A salad of shrimps and oysters. Beef in *casserole,* stuffed chicken, a salad of the season, variety of cheeses, a special cream and fruits. *Ouzo, Rose* and *Mavrodaphni* wine at the end.

For Easter the menu includes :

As appetizers *kokoretsi* and red eggs.
As main dish : Lamb on the spit, or baked, potatoes and spring salad.
As a dessert ice cream and fruits.

For Christmas the menu includes the traditional stuffed turkey or a baked poultry dish. An *avgolemono* soup is very welcome to open and a salad of the season, potatoes and a variety of cheeses to accompany the poultry dish. A special cake is baked for the occasion served with fruits and coffee. A shrimp cocktail or lobster with mayonnaise or a variety of *meze* can substitute for the *avgolemono* soup.

On New Year's eve Greeks usually serve appetizers, baked poultry, potatoes, cabbage salad and a pudding. Or they prepare a buffet dinner—if they have many guests with a variety of *meze, spanakopitta,* fruit jelly and the traditional stuffed turkey. The main attraction, of course, is the cutting of the *vassilopitta* served with *diples,* fruits, coffee and liquor.

Having an important guest for dinner gives the opportunity to a housewife to demonstrate her talent in the kitchen as well as in the setting of a banquet. A strict etiquette is applied in preparing the table and decorating it. The menu usualy includes baked fish and baked lamb, or boiled fish and baked beef. Or it may consist of steak with artichokes and squash prepared in butter or poultry with a season salad and a variety of cheeses. In case fish is eliminated, a spaghetti dish may substitute, but never both. Coffee and fruits are a must, of course. A

Greek housewife never tries to overdo it in a formal banquet. She concentrates on good quality of the ingredients and a delightful taste of the preparations and keeps the banquet light to the stomach.

For the lent season the Greek housewife gets a span of breath as most of the menus consist of ready made food stuff. She will prepare, of course, the traditional *taramosalata* to last for days, and some *dolmadakia* with rice, and will alternate with a dish of artichokes *a la polita* and some octopus boiled and served with olive oil and lemon juice or cooked with rice. A spaghetti dish prepared with olive oil also provides a variety in the monotony of the *nistisima*—the fasting season menus. The rest consists of olives, halva, oysters, pickled vegetables, salads and fruit salads. A few types of vegetable pies are baked with olive oil and served during the lent season in various areas of the Greek country side.

Coming to the everyday headache Greek housewives have divided their daily menus according to the seasons. In springtime, for instance, they will fry or bake fish on Wednesdays and Fridays and will add a *pilafi* with peas, and will insist on a *skordalia* sauce with fried squash on alternate Fridays. Spring is the best season for *skordalia*. A spaghetti and egg dish will do on Mondays and a cube steak dinner on Tuesday accompanied with a *spanakopitta*. Thursday calls for artichokes au gratin and a *kima* dish and Saturday is a good day for an olive oil dish, *briam* or some other vegetable and fried lamb livers. Sunday, of course, is a meat day and either lamb fricasse or *exohiko* are in order, with a pastry to sweeten the weekend.

In summertime Greek housewives make their menus very light. Vegetable dishes, omelets, fish preparations, salads, *feta* cheese and a *kapama* for Sunday, make the job easy. An occasional *pilafi* is added and, when I mention salads I include, of course, the *taramosalata* and *melitzanosalata*.

In fall, light soups of vegetables, tomato and *trahana* are added to the daily menus. Fried fish and squids with spinach make a Wednesday or Friday dinner welcome. A *saganaki* can be an added attraction and some *keftedes* of meat or potatoes and squash. Here and there a *tyropitta* can make the dinner complete and a salad of boiled potatoes with plenty olive oil, lemon juice, sprinkled with parsley is also a fresh addition.

Heavier soups, navy beans, lentils, vegetable and others, dominate the wintertime menus. Spinach with rice is also a favored first dish. Meat and fish and poultry are cooked with a rich sauce, *yahni* or *plaki*.

Of course these are just some tips in solving the problem of the daily menu in case your people are used or like Greek cookery so much, they would adopt it as a daily menu with pleasure.

INDEX OF RECIPES

	Pages			*Pages*
Almond Cake	160	Bagels		157
Almond Crispies	152	Wine *Must*	157	
Amygdalota	152	*Bakaliaros*		
Angel Food Cake	157	Vrastos	126	
Anginares		Skordalia	126	
A La Polita	62	*Baklavas*		143
Tiganites	65	*Bamies*		70
Me Koukia	65	Beans		
Gemistes	66	Salad	43	
Au Gratin	66	Soup	47	
Salata	67	Stew	69	
Antidia Avgolemono	73	*Bechamel*		37
Apple Compote	169	Beef-Onion Stew		97
Arni		Bitter Orange		166
Psito	91	Rolled	167	
Pilafi	91	*Bougatsa*		150
Fricasse	92	Bouillabaisse		51
Giuvetsi Hilopites	92	Bows		148
Kokkinisto	93	*Briam*		58
Exohiko	93	Broth		53
Horiatiko	94			
Sti Souvla	94			
Artichokes		Cabbage Stuffed		73
In Oil	62	Cauliflower		
Fried	65	Oil-Tomato	72	
With Fava Beans	65	Au Gratin	72	
Stuffed	66	Cheese		
Au Gratin	66	Flaming	29	
Salad	67	Triangles	29	
Astakos Mayoneza	130	Cherry Syrup		170
Athenian Style Fish	125	Chestnut Stuffing		105
Athinaiki Mayoneza	125	Chicken		
Avgolemono		Soup	48	
Sauce	36	Pilaf	107	
Soupa	47	With Noodles	107	
Kolokithia	59	Stew	108	
Antidia	73	Grilled	108	
		Fricasse	109	
		Oregano	109	
Baby Eggplant	167	Stuffed	110	

With Yoghourt	110	Fassolakia Yahni	68
Pie	111	Fassolia	
Chick-Pea Soup	50	Salata	43
Christmas Bread	156	Yahni	69
Christopsomo	156	Fava	50
Codfish		Fava Beans Artichokes	65
Boiled	126	Fides	49
Garlic Sauce	126	Fish	
Compotes		Soup	51
Apple	169	Boiled	121
Quince	169	Broiled	121
Copenhagen	158	Spetsiota	122
Cream Karamele	162	Stew	123
Custard Pie		With Lemon	123
Galatoboureko	144	Wine Sauce	123
Bougatsa	150	Marine	124
Custard Wine Must	162	Savoury	124
		Mayonnaise Athenian Style	125
Diples	148	Fish Roe	
Dolmades	30	Salad	42
Me Lahano	73	Patties	133
Domates		Flaming Cheese	29
Gemistes	67	Floyeres	148
Omeleta	68	Fricasse	
		Lamb	92
		Arni	92
Easter		Chicken	109
Soup	54	Kotopoulo	109
Lamb	94	Fritters	151
Bread	156	Squash	60
Cake	156	Potato	71
Egg and Lemon			
Sauce	36	Galatoboureko	144
Soup	47	Galopoula Gemisti	111
Stuffed Squash	59	Garides	
Endives	73	Pilafi I	85
Eggplant		Pilafi II	127
Salad	41	Tiganites	128
Fried	61	Yahni	128
Skordalia	61	Garlic Sauce	38
Stew	62	Giant Beans Oil-Tomato	69
In Oil	63	Gigantes Plaki	69
Slippers	63	Giuvetsi	81
Pie	64	Arni Hilopites	92
Baby, Spoon Sweet	167	Greens Boiled	74
Endives Egg-Lemon	73	Ground Beef and Macaroni Pie	98
		Gyros	95
Faki	48		
Fassolada	47	Halva	149

Halvas		149	*Kombosta*	
Hare with Onions		101	Milo	169
Hilopites			Kydoni	169
Giuvetsi		92	*Kotopitta*	111
Kotopoulo		107	*Kotopoulo*	
Honey			Pilafi	107
Puffs		149	Me Hilopites	107
Pie		161	Kapama	108
Horiatiki		41	Tis Sharas	108
Horta			Fricasse	109
Salata		43	Riganato	109
Vrasta		74	Gemisto	110
Hortosoupa		53	Me Yaourti	110
Htapodhi			*Kotosoupa*	48
Pilafi I		86	*Koukia Anginares*	65
Pilafi II		131	*Koulourakia*	157
Krasato		131	*Kounoupidi*	
Htenia Pilafi		127	Yahni	72
			Au Gratin	72
			Kourabiedes	146
Imam-Baildi		63	*Kreatopitta*	99
			Krema Karamele	162
			Kritharaki	80
			Ksifias Souvlaki	126
Jellied Pig		99	*Kydoni*	
			Kofto	165
			Pelte	166
Kakavia		51	*Kydonopasto*	165
Kalamaria				
Tiganita		129		
Pilafi		129		
Gemista		130	*Ladolemono*	36
Kapama		97	*Ladoxido*	35
Arni		97	*Lagos Stifatho*	101
Moshari		97	*Lahano Me Dolmades*	73
Kotopoulo		108	Lamb	
Karydopitta		160	Roast	91
Kataifi		145	Pilaf	91
Kefalaki		95	Baked with Noodles	92
Keftedes		30	Fricasse	92
Kokoretsi		96	Braised	93
Kolokithakia Salata		57	Roast in Paper	93
Kolokithia			Baked Peasant Style	94
Tiganita		57	Easter	94
Yahni		57	On-A-Spit	95
Gemista		58	Lamb's	
Avgolemono		59	Head	95
Souffle		60	"Sausage"	96
Papoutsakia		61	*Lambropsomo*	156
Kolokithokeftedes		60	Lentil Soup	48
Kolokithopitta		59	Liver with Sauce	100
Kopenhaghi		158	Lobster Mayonnaise	130

Loukoumades	149	Octopus		
Loukoumaki	170	With Rice	86	
		With Rice II	131	
		In Wine	131	
Macaroni and Ground Beef Stew	98	Okra		70
Makaronada	77	Olive Oil		
Makaronia		And Vinegar Sauce	35	
Au Gratin	79	And Lemon Sauce	36	
Me Bacon	80	Olives with Partridges		116
Marin Fish	124	*Ortikia*		
Mastic	168	Pilafi	115	
Mastiha	168	Sharas	115	
Mayeritsa	54	Orzo		80
Mayoneza	38	With Meat	81	
Mayonnaise	38			
Meat				
Balls	30	*Pantespani*		157
With Orzo	81	*Papoutsakia Melitzanes*		63
Stew	97	Patridges		
Rice Balls	98	Salmi	116	
Pie	99	With Olives	116	
Loaf	100	Pasta Soup		52
Melitzanaki	167	*Pasticcio*		
Melitzanes		I	79	
Tiganites	61	II	98	
Stifatho	62	*Patates Yahni*		70
Papoutsakia	63	*Patatokeftedes*		71
Melitzanosalata	41	*Patatosalata*		43
Melomakarouna	147	*Patsas*		54
Melopitta	161	Patties Fish Roe		133
Midia Pilafi	132	Peppers Stuffed		68
Migdalopitta	160	*Perdikes*		
Minced Meat Stuffing	105	Salmi	116	
Mixed Salad	41	Me Elies	116	
Mixed Vegetables Baked	58	*Pestrofa Riganati*		124
Moussaka	64	Phoenicean Honey Cakes		147
Moustalevria	162	Pig Jellied		99
Moustokouloura	157	Pigeons Tomato Sauce		117
Mussels with Rice	132	*Pikti*		99
		Pilaf		
		Rice	85	
Nerantzaki	166	Lamb	91	
Nerantzi Gyristo	167	With Chicken	107	
New Year's Cake	155	*Pilafi*		85
Noodles		Me Garides	85	
With Lamb	91	Htapodhi	86	
With Chicken	107	Arni	91	
Nut		Kotopoulo	107	
Cake	159	Ortikia	115	
Rolls	159	Htenia	127	

Garides II	127	Roast Lamb		91
Kalamaria	129	Rose Petals		168
Htapodhi II	131	*Roulo*		100
Midia	132			
Piperies Gemistes	68			
Pitsounia Yahni	117	*Saganaki*		29
Porgies with Celery	125	*Salingaria Yahni*		132
Potato		Salmi		
Salad	43	Partridges	116	
Fritters	71	Perdikes	116	
Potatoes Oil-Tomato	70	*Saltsa Tomata*		37
Poutingha	151	*Saraili*		159
Psari		*Savaren*		159
Vrasto	121	*Savoro Psari*		124
Sharas	121	Savoury Fish		124
Spetsiota	122	Scallops with Rice		127
Plaki	123	*Scaltsounia*		152
Lemonato	123	*Shish Kebab*		96
Krasato	123	Shrimps		
Marinato	124	With Rice	85	
Savoro	124	With Rice II	127	
Psarosoupa	51	Fried	128	
Pudding	151	Braised	128	
		Sikotakia Saltsa		100
		Skordalia		38
Quail		Eggplant	61	
White Rice	115	Bakaliaros	126	
Grilled	115	Slippers		
Quince		Squash	61	
Grated	165	Eggplant	63	
Paste	165	Snails Stewed		132
Puree	166	Sour Cherry		166
Compote	169	*Souvlaki*		96
		Souvlas Arni		94
		Spaghetti		77
Ravani	158	Chopped Meat	79	
Revithia	50	Au Gratin	79	
Rice		Timbale	80	
Spinach	71	*Spanakopitta*		31
Pilaf	85	*Spanakorizo*		71
Shrimps	85	Spinach		
Octopus	86	Pie	31	
Stuffing	106	With Rice	71	
Quail	115	Squids		
Scallops	127	Fried	129	
Shrimps II	127	With Rice	129	
Squids	129	Stuffed	130	
Octopus II	131	Squash		
Mussels	132	Boiled	57	
Pudding	161	Fried	57	
Rizogalo	161	Stew	57	

Stuffed	58		*Triantafilo*	168
Stuffed Egg Lemon	59		Tripe Soup	54
Pie	59		Trout Oregano	124
Fritters	60		*Tsipoura Selino*	125
Souffle	60		*Tsoureki*	156
Slippers	61		Turkey Stuffed	111
Stifadho			*Tzatziki*	42
Melitzanes	62			
Moshari	97			
Arni	97		*Vanilla*	168
Lagos	101		*Vassilopitta*	155
String Beans in Oil		68	Vegetables	
Stuffed			Boiled	43
Vine Leaves	30		Soup	53
Tomatoes	67		Baked Mixed	58
Cabbage	73		Vermicelli	49
Turkey	111		Vine Leafs Stuffed	30
Rolls	148		*Vissinada*	170
Stuffing			*Vissino*	166
Minced Meat	105			
Chestnut	105			
Rice	106		Walnut Pie	160
Svigoi		150	Wheat Pudding	151
Swordfish on Skewer		126	White Sauce	37
			Wine Must	
			Bagels	157
Tahini Soup		52	Custard	162
Tahinosoupa		52		
Taramokeftedes		133		
Taramosalata		42	*Yaourti Me Kotopoulo*	110
Tiganites		151	*Yaourtopitta*	161
Timbale Spaghetti		80	Yellow Lentil Soup	50
Tiropitakia		29	Yoghourt	
Tiropitta		29	Salad	42
Tomato			With Chicken	110
Sauce	37		Pie	161
Soup	49		*Yuvarlakia*	98
Omelet	68			
Tomatosoupa		49		
Trahana		52	*Zoumi*	53
Triangles Cheese		29		

CONTENTS

Foreword 5
Introduction 7

Part I WELCOME

Discovering Petros 11
From The Streets of Athens 13
Say "Opaa" When You Think Greek Food 16
World's Most Honored Restaurant 17
Scholar's Comments 18
I'd Rather Have a Cook 19
Learned Men at Supper 21
Eating By The Calendar 23

Part II KALI OREXI

An Essay on *Meze* 27
Adventure in Herbs 33
The Notorious *Saltsades* 35
Love of Salads 39
Speaking of Soups 45
Going Vegetarian 55
Getting Fat 75
The Spaghetti 77
The *Pilafas* 83

Part III "ELA STO PSITO"

"Ela Sto Psito" 89
Those Wonderful Flying Creatures 103
Stuffing 105
"Diana's Foresters" 113
Those Marvelous Swimmers 119

Part IV THE TRIPTYCH

The Triptych 137
For Your Sweet Tooth 139

185

Get *Filo* 141
Bake A Cake 153
Wish Me *Hronia Polla* 163

Part V EPILOGUE

Inner Sanctum 173
Is Ygeian 175
The Daily Headache 177
Index of Recipes 179

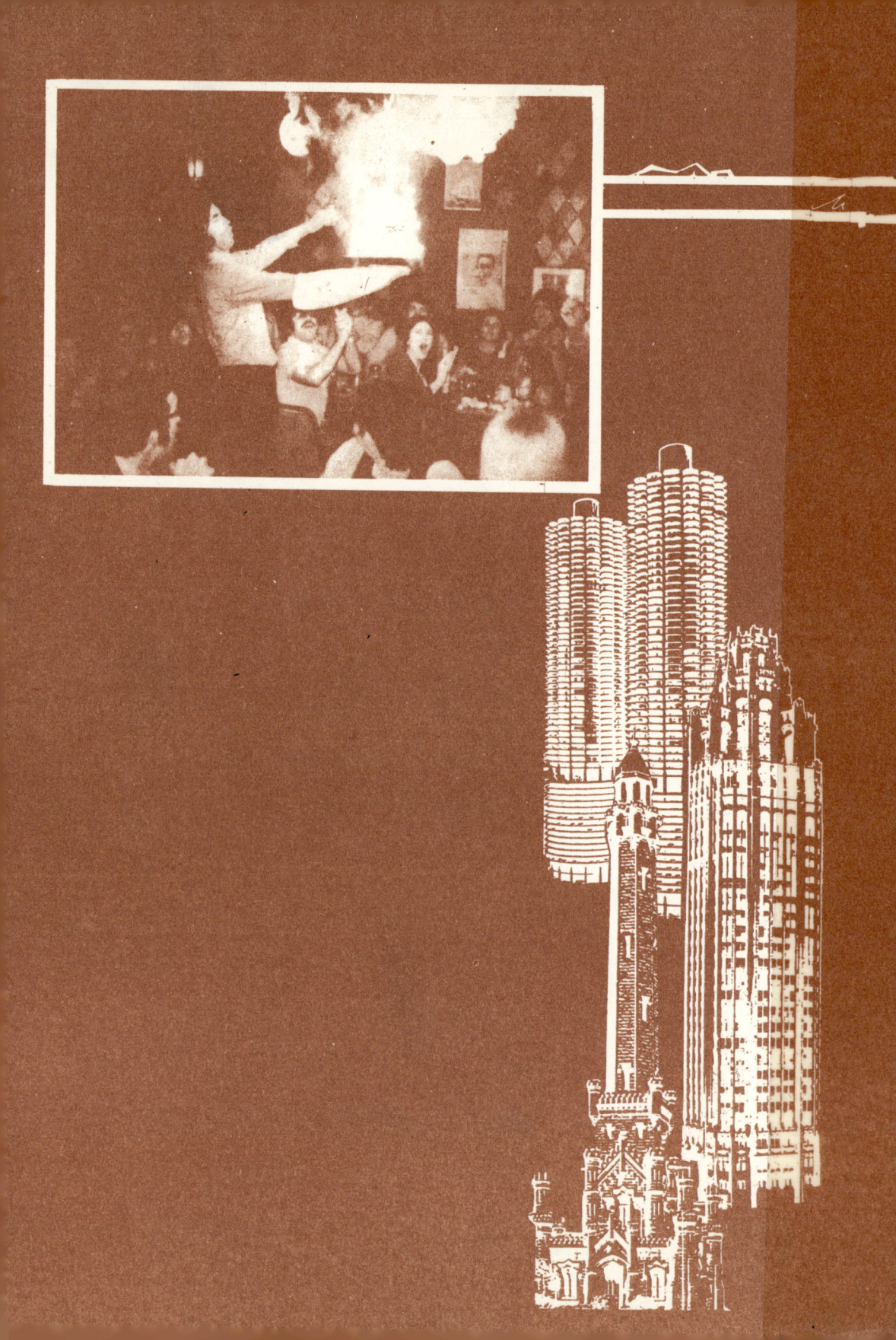